The New Restaurant Manager

ISBN 978-1-7364219-2-5
E-book ISBN 978-1-7364219-1-8

THE NEW RESTAURANT MANAGER

HOW TO GET AHEAD, AVOID ROOKIE MISTAKES, AND STILL HAVE A LIFE

John T. Self, PhD

Professor of Hospitality Management

Former Manager trainee, Assistant manager, General manager,
Vice president of operations, Restaurant owner

CONTENTS

PART 4:
TOMORROW IS ALMOST HERE

INTRODUCTION

Fools learn from their own mistakes.
Wise men learn from the mistakes of others.

—GEORGE BERNARD SHAW

W hy not learn from the mistakes of others? This book is for the thousands of new restaurant managers beginning their careers who will make the same mistakes that thousands of other managers made, just like I did when I started. The bad news is that these mistakes will predictably happen; the good news is that they don't have to happen.

This book is written to help beginning restaurant managers in general and beginning chain restaurant managers in particular. The world of chain restaurant management has its own set of rules, culture, and expectations that few new managers are prepared for, even if they had been a restaurant employee before. Some managers survive these mistakes, and some do not. To make this worse, some in upper management actually believe that this sink or swim mentality works as a great weeding out process and would not change it even though their restaurants would be far better off if rookie manager mistakes could be reduced.

The same mistakes that I made when I was a new restaurant manager are exactly the same mistakes that new restaurant managers are still making today. Later, when I became a general manager, I saw my new assistant managers make the same mistakes and later, when I changed careers into university teaching, I continued to hear about these same mistakes being made by my students after they graduated.

Traditionally, the only way new managers got to be experienced managers was by making mistakes, some serious, and some not so serious. Mentors would help, but unfortunately, most managers don't have the luxury of having a mentor warn them of potential mistakes to avoid, how to handle situations, how to spot warning signs before situations turn serious, or how to stay focused instead of drifting off.

This book takes you through the beginning stage of your career when you are most vulnerable to making mistakes because of your lack of experience. The book goes through common situations, scenarios, and events that you are likely to experience at the beginning stage of your career. It also goes a step further by taking the long view, rather than just getting through a shift.

By considering the most common situations and decision points in your beginning career, rookie managers like yourself can avoid common mistakes and accelerate your career.

This book is the result of years of personal experience in restaurant management, teaching restaurant management, observing new restaurant managers, and gathering solid expertise from all levels of restaurant management. The personal experiences that the author had, both good and bad, and the experiences that he has observed have proven to be the same experiences that every single new restaurant manager goes through.

This is a career, self-improvement book that will accelerate the learning curve of new managers and prevent bad decisions and questionable career moves that can derail or delay promising careers. This is written in a practical, down to earth writing style to help new restaurant managers begin their career journeys.

PART 1

You Got
This!

CHAPTER 1

HOW YOU REALLY GET PROMOTED

Promotions don't just happen.
You make them happen.

Whether you made it into management directly from college or worked your way up from employee, congratulations. Now that you've got a management position, your next step is to make the most of the opportunity and move onward and upward.

Getting into management brings an entirely different set of problems and challenges requiring a different mindset as you transition from student or employee. Your reputation begins the day you step foot in the restaurant as a manager trainee. It is vital that you establish a pattern of success starting that first day to build your personal credibility.

The purpose of this book is to reduce the pain and length of this transition period while you learn what is expected of you and the skills necessary for success. By not falling into common traps and mistakes, your momentum can accelerate, rather than stall. Your journey to promotion really begins when you start contributing back to the company.

Now that you are in management, your first big career goal will be to get promoted to general manager in a restaurant or food and beverage director in a hotel. Depending on the company, there are probably 2 to 5 times more assistant managers than general managers with every assistant manager wanting to be promoted. Your primary and overarching goal is to break out of the pack of assistant managers by differentiating yourself. This is not just separating yourself from your fellow assistants, it is about separating yourself from ALL the other assistants. Here's how to do it.

PRIMARY TRUTH

The key person that controls your promotion from assistant manager to GM is your very own General Manager. The GM calls all the shots and, at least regarding your career, the GM is the most important person in your world right now. The importance of this person to your career cannot be overstated. This is the one person that you must impress, earn their confidence, and have in your corner.

I have always thought that this promotion, from assistant manager to general manager is the toughest promotion of them all. One reason is that the general manager gets a lot of face time with the area manager or above, assistant managers get very little face time with anyone else other than the general manager. So, that means that most information about assistants come from the general manager and filtered through the general manager, both good and bad. Your GM can make you look really, really good, or really, really bad.

HOW PROMOTIONS WORK IN A TYPICAL CHAIN

An opening for a general manager comes up in your region. Your area manager (district manager or supervisor in some chains, other names in other chains) asks each of his/her general managers if they have any assistant managers who are ready to be promoted to general manager. Each general manager then pitches any of their assistant managers who they feel are ready to be promoted. The general manager who makes the strongest and most passionate case for their assistant will usually get the assistant promoted.

Curve Ball: Obviously, GM's who have the most influence with their district manager are more likely to get their assistants promoted over assistant managers of other GM's. Usually, they got this influence from managing restaurants that were doing really well or they have a long-standing relationship with the district manager. So, if you are unfortunate enough to be with a restaurant that is under-performing or a GM who is out of favor with the area manager, you could be at a disadvantage. This situation can be overcome but it is more difficult for the assistant who winds up in one of the worst units. In this case, you should work on being more visible to your area manager and making your department the best. You shouldn't overreact, get depressed, or immediately ask for a transfer; just recognize you'll have to work to overcome this disadvantage.

The good news is that General Managers want their assistants to get promoted because developing assistant managers into general managers is a key factor for GM's themselves to get promoted. Management development is extremely important in a general manager's career, so there is strong career motivation for the GM to get their assistants promoted.

OPPORTUNITY + READINESS = PROMOTION

This is one factor that you **do** have control over. You've got to be ready when the opportunity happens and this only happens by doing a great job every day, regardless of what happens in your personal life.

I've seen several assistant managers (and general managers) who would have gotten promoted, but they started doing their job on autopilot. They weren't doing a bad job but were not working beyond their shift. Their performance dipped and of course that's when the promotion opportunity came. Be consistent every day because your behavior is noticed. One very good way to combat this is to have weekly goals that you want to accomplish. We'll discuss that more in the Work Your Shift chapter.

That's why starting your quest for GM must be planned out and intentional, not left to chance. You want to build a relationship with your GM by directly stating your career goals to your GM. Have you given your GM all the ammunition that he needs to convince an area manager that you are ready? Have you been consistent and dependable? Have you met or exceeded your budget numbers? These areas will be covered along with how you can actually get them done.

The bottom line is that assistant managers who are promoted have impressed their General Manager as being focused and serious about work. Your restaurant probably does between $2 million and $15 million per year in sales. Every dollar flows through unit management. That's why upper management wants management they can trust to do a good job today and a better job tomorrow. They want someone who sees the restaurant as a whole, takes the job seriously, and if they don't know something, finds out.

The best way to begin this is to have a career plan. This gives you a map of where you want to go in your career, your timetable, and what you must do to get there. It shows where you are weak and what to do about the weaknesses. The career plan helps you to be the player on the sideline who goes to the coach and says "let me in, let me in" while other players are content to just sit on the bench and wait to be called. Each player sends a clear message. Which message are you sending?

QUICK THOUGHT

Managers who get promoted and managers who don't get promoted spend roughly the same amount of time in the restaurant. So, if you're going to be there anyway, work hard, work smart, take your work seriously, and work toward specific goals. It is better to be promoted than not be promoted.

SO, WHAT DO YOU HAVE TO DO TO GET PROMOTED?

1: Your GM is key

Your immediate boss is by far the most important factor in your promotion. Here's why. In a typical restaurant chain, each restaurant has one GM and 2 to 11 assistant managers. The GM's boss is usually a District Manager who oversees 3 to 5 General Managers. Unfortunately, your exposure to the district manager will be limited, but your GM probably has some form of daily contact along with regular personal visits to the restaurant.

When an opening for a GM position becomes available, the district managers will be asked to name any assistant managers in their district who are ready to be promoted. How does the District Manager know who these assistant managers are? The GM's tell the District Manager who they believe are ready.

That is why the GM is so significant for you. If he becomes your champion, you will get promoted. If the GM does not speak out strongly for you to the district manager, it is much more difficult for you, basically impossible. If the GM speaks badly of you, you have no chance of being promoted. Hopefully, when you are ready, your GM will push strongly for you to be promoted to the district manager.

The good news is that getting assistant managers promoted is very, very good for general managers. When an assistant gets promoted, it is a big deal for a GM because it shows that the GM has done a good job with developing managers. This is an essential trait for a general manager to have before they can be promoted.

> *The function of leadership is to produce*
> *more leaders, not more followers.*
> -RALPH NADER

2: Your employees are key

Once you're a manager, you can't do it all yourself; for maybe the first time, you must rely on others. This can be a tough transition, especially for new managers who came from employee because the rules change. Instead of focusing on yourself, you must now focus on other employees. You leave a world where being good at your job was in your control and black and white, to a subjective, gray world where you are dependent on customers and employees to be successful.

No matter how good you were as an employee, you now enter unknown territory. This may sound strange since you were around management every day, but employees are not aware of the many interlocking parts required to have a smooth shift, just as even good assistant managers don't fully grasp the GM's responsibilities until they live it. Managers must see the entire restaurant rather than just one part, go from being technically excellent in one part to a position that can seem overwhelming.

Not every employee makes this transition successfully. Some realize quickly that management is not for them and go back to being a confident, valuable employee. Others struggle to make the transition with much dependent on how good their company is with development. Management is not an easy, intuitive skill. It takes experience, some hand holding, and patience. Not everyone is suited to a position that involves hundreds of decisions every day. I remember going home after shifts and telling my wife that I didn't want to make any decisions. Movie? Great. Chicken or pasta? Yes.

3: Getting promoted is not how good a job you do as assistant manager.

This may seem counter intuitive, but most important is whether your general manager perceives that you can do the job of general manager. Does the general manager still see you as an employee or assistant manager, or as a general manager? Can the GM talk with you as a peer, discussing sales, budgets, costs, turnover, and the other hundreds of things that a general manager oversees? Once your GM perceives you as a GM, you're almost there.

4: Results count, effort doesn't.

Many new managers believe that working long hours, coming in when you're not scheduled, coming in way before your shift, and staying late will be impressive. The truth is that it is not. Effort does not make up for not meeting your budget. Yes, putting in all those hours does show effort and maybe even strong effort, but if you are not getting the job done, so what?

New managers get really frustrated and angry when they get criticized over missed budgets after having put in a huge number of hours, sacrificed time with their families and friends to work those hours. But the bottom line is that if you're not meeting budget, just putting in long hours does not change the fact that you're not meeting your budget.

The answer is that you've got to change something. Putting in more hours is not the answer. So, rather than get frustrated, concentrate on why you're having problems, put together a game plan, and solve it. Don't rely on effort alone to give you some slack. Don't hesitate to ask for help to make sure you're on the right track. Find out which units are doing the best in each area and go there, call them or email them for advice. It is far better to ask for help than continue to struggle. When you have the resources to ask for help, ask. This is smart management. Not asking for help when it is available is dumb management.

> **CAUTION.** Do not seek help until you've put together an action plan yourself. Think it through and do the best job possible. Then, and only then, are you ready to seek help. You've got to show your GM that you have put in effort rather than just ask for help.

5: Promotable managers anticipate and prevent problems, not just put out fires.

If you always just react, you'll never get control.

-KEVIN KELLY, FORMER VP OF OPERATIONS,
VP OF DEVELOPMENT, FARMER BOYS BURGERS

This is why you get the big bucks. The average manager puts out fires. The promotable manager *prevents* fires from happening in the first place. Too many managers are great at putting out fires, but not so good at preventing the fires in the first place. I am convinced that the reason some managers like putting out fires is that it makes them feel good. How boring to prevent a problem. For example, if you have an employee that is coughing, sneezing, and constantly blowing her nose, there is a good chance that employee will be calling in sick tomorrow. So instead of just offering a Kleenex, it would be a good idea to ask the servers present if anyone could work tomorrow if needed. The servers are there to ask, there is no panic, no urgency, and you will probably be successful having someone willing to come in if called. Not only is this smart management, this will give you major points with your other managers for heading off a potentially tough situation the next day. Even if the employee doesn't call in sick, the other managers will appreciate your actions. This will pay off big time if (when) the GM asks the other assistants if you take care of them before and after shifts. You're sending a great message that the GM will hear loud and clear. Just be consistent.

It is so easy to get lulled into putting out fires. It feels so good to run around, issuing orders, and making things happen. At first glance, or to an outsider, this type of manager is the kind that often gets rave compliments: appearing so active, so useful, so productive. But such activity can be misleading.

Putting-out-the-fires-of-crisis management feels good. A problem appears and you solve it. It does feel good to be the cavalry and ride in to save the town from burning. But, too often, you get tied up in one thing so as you were saving the town from burning, the bank was robbed and your horse was stolen.

Too often not enough emphasis is placed on preventing crises in the first place. The lesson should be that the more fires you have to put out, the worse job that management has done. Management's job is to be proactive, anticipating and preventing, rather than reactive, waiting until the problem bites you.

One "problem" with the preventing and anticipating style of management is that it is simply less glamorous when compared to the style of the crisis manager. Managers aren't running around, they're calm. But the payoff for a preventing manager is a smooth shift. Your employees will also resent you "saving the day" when you should have been ahead of the problems. But smooth days have the important side effect of allowing the preventive manager to accomplish more than the crisis manager: they simply have more time to do more and are doing so in a much less stressful environment.

Warning: Because your shifts are smooth, some employees won't see what made them smooth and will only see that you are not stressed and think that you're not doing much. To combat this, get to know the key players (the employees who the GM respects and listens to) and make sure you casually talk to them during the shifts about some of the things that you did to make the shift go smoothly and with apparently no effort. This will head off them telling the GM that you don't do much and have easy shifts. Not everyone recognizes that 'easy' shifts rarely come without good management.

6: Stay focused on your area of responsibility

Many of us tend to focus on the parts of the job that we like, rather than stay with our core job. It is easy to get distracted or spend time in another area especially when asked to help. Hospitality managers by nature want to help. But, before you offer to spend time helping in another area, make damn sure your area is in great shape. Maybe you really get into programming the POS. You're really good at it, but it is not in your area. If helping would force you to spend a lot of time away from your primary duties, just say no. But, of course, if the GM asks you to do it, that's another story. A better alternative might be to volunteer to give a POS workshop to the other assistants. This could show the GM not only are you good in programming but that you're a team player willing to share your time and knowledge.

Keeping focused on your area will prevent you from having your priorities questioned if your area is not so good. Why did you spend time away from your area when your own area needs attention? You might answer that you were just trying to help, but again, your sense of priorities will come into question. Most of us in the industry want to help others, just make sure helping does not take away from effort in your own area. It is great to be good at something and willing to help, but keep in mind that if your area is not 100% good, then your priority is to your own area.

7: Accept personal responsibility

Don't make excuses about anything. Don't blame anyone or anything else. If you've screwed up, you screwed up. Own it. Your priority is to make sure you don't do it again. Don't be defensive. If you are being criticized for something that you did not do well, just listen, learn, and don't do it again. This is one time to just listen. In most cases, anything you say will come out wrong.

8: Have a career plan

This is so important it has its own chapter. Getting promoted doesn't just happen. It is not fate. You have to take control of your own career. You're the one who has to make it happen. If you don't have a plan, it's like being on a raft and letting the river take you where it wants instead of having a tiller with you deciding where you want to go. See Career Plan chapter for more.

9: Do more than expected

This sounds so obvious, but it doesn't always happens. For example, if you are in charge of cleaning, make sure it is done well. I've seen some GM's who will intentionally hide $20 bills in places that should have been cleaned to check whether you have or have not done a good job.

10: Know the score

This is also so important that it has its own chapter. If you've had a performance evaluation, take a hard look at it. Have you worked on each of your "needs work" items? Does your GM know that you have worked on them, and, more importantly, can your GM see a difference? Once you've started working on any weaknesses, make it a point to be consistent. It is important to know how does your GM and your peers see you? Most of us have a very high perception of ourselves, but what is this reality? See Know the Score chapter for more.

11: Differentiate yourself, get out of the pile of assistant managers, and get your GM to view you as promotable. (See this entire book).

12: Act and dress the part.

This means that what you wear, your posture, and your attitude are important; otherwise, your customers, employees, and especially your GM will never take you seriously.

MYTH: YOU MUST BE THE BEST AT EVERY POSITION

Definitely not. But you need to know and understand each position well enough that you could train someone how to do it, evaluate how they are doing, and fill in temporarily if needed, or you just want to. Speed is not as important as knowing the mechanics of each position. If you are the perfectionist type, fight the urge.

WHAT WOULD YOU DO?

You were just contacted by the home office that one of your employees was overpaid $500 on their last paycheck. They said that it was a mistake and want you to get the money back to correct the situation.

How would you approach the employee? What if he had already spent it?

WHAT I DID

When this happened, I thought it was unrealistic to collect the full $500 at one time, so I pushed back on the home office. After all, it was their mistake. I proposed that the home office agree to deduct a small amount (something like a maximum of $50) from the employee's paycheck until it was paid off rather than insisting that the entire amount be paid off immediately. If the employee cannot pay their bills, the employee will have no choice but to quit.

REFLECTION

Sure, the employee should have said something about the amount since it was a lot over his normal paycheck. But he spent it and probably thought it may go unnoticed. (Doesn't happen).

Overall, I wouldn't do anything different here. Sometimes you have to go to bat for your employees. To me, the options were simple: either the employee gets a small amount deducted from each paycheck and the employee can still pay his bills or the home office demands the entire amount, which would mean we would lose an employee and the company would not get any money back.

In this case, the home office agreed to the reduced amount and we kept our employee.

CHAPTER 2

WORK THE SHIFT

Don't let the shift work you

If you're reading this book, you obviously care about your career. One important element in your career is how you do day-to-day in working your shifts. What you do (or don't do) during your shifts are super important.

Many managers think of shifts as something to get through. But, realistically, when you think about it, what you do during your shift each day adds up to your career. That's why it is so important to use each shift to move your career forward rather than just be a series of days that might (or might not) get you promoted.

Many managers tend to put their energy into the busiest part of the shift because that's when they feel a sense of importance and urgency, but when the rush is over, they relax. This is understandable, but they're wasting a great opportunity to get a lot done that would get them out earlier in the short term and advance their career in the long term.

Consider this:

Good and bad managers, effective and lazy managers, all work about the same number of hours. So, if you're going to be at work anyway, make the most of it. I guarantee you that you will be promoted much sooner than the manager who only puts in minimum effort. The benefits to you include smooth shifts, respect from your employees, and a career that takes care of itself.

CHECKLISTS ARE YOUR BEST FRIEND

When I first started as an assistant manager, I regularly forgot something when I closed or opened. Usually, it would be something relatively minor, like forgetting to check one of the server-side duties. But sometimes it would be important, like forgetting to place an order. This was massively hurting my chances of being taken seriously for promotion. After a particularly bad chewing out by my GM, I resolved that this would never happen again.

The answer for me was the lowly checklist. Pilots use checklists every time they go up even when they have flown the same airplane hundreds of times. The reason they use them is because they work! Nothing is forgotten. I resolved to use a checklist for everything. I used them when I opened, when I closed, when I did a line check, did inventory, everything. If there wasn't one, I made one. When there was one, I customized it.

Most restaurants use checklists for line checks, opening and closing. But even when there is a checklist provided, customize it to add extra things that you want to get done.

The bottom line? I never forgot anything again and I could leave knowing everything was done. Use checklists!

TO THINK LIKE A GM, YOU HAVE TO KNOW WHAT THE GM KNOWS

When you first come in for your shift, make it a habit to write down key figures about how your restaurant is doing. The physical act of writing the numbers down will help lock it in. Looking at these numbers each shift will make the restaurant come alive and you will be more aware of the entire restaurant, not just your department. When you know these figures, you can better understand the general manager's perspective. This will help you understand the challenges and successes of the entire restaurant making you look like a promotable manager.

Many assistants never take the time or trouble to look beyond their own department. Keeping this information top of mind keeps you thinking like a GM and able to talk with the GM about trends, such as sales going way over or under budget, or how you're going to reduce the dining room supplies because of a sales decline. This is definitely promotable manager material.

Every shift write the following on a 3x5 card, phone, or hand, whatever is easiest to refer to:

1. The actual month to date (MTD) sales, budgeted sales for the month, and your sales projection for the month. This sales projection is an important figure as it gives you a heads up to adjust your spending during the month so that you can meet budget.

Here's how to get the sales projection:

Wait a full 7 days so the slow days and busy days of the week are included.

• To get the projected Month-to-Date (MTD) sales- starting on the 8th day of the month, add up the first 7 days of sales.

• Then divide by 7 to get the average daily sales.

• Then multiply this average daily sale by the number of days in the month.

• This gives you a projection of how much total sales you'll do for the month. It won't be perfect, but it will give you an idea of how the month is going. This gets more accurate with each passing day and helps you adjust how you spend your budget better during the month.

2. The MTD labor of your area against budget. Use the same technique above.

3. The MTD of your other areas of responsibility, like supplies.

The three points above keep you aware of how the sales of the whole restaurant is doing (thinking like a GM) plus keeping you aware of how you are doing in controlling your individual responsibilities. This also makes it easy to discuss with the GM the problems and the opportunities of the restaurant each month.

4. The one goal, task, or project that you want to accomplish during your shift that is over and above running your shift.

5. During the shift, write down the names of employees you notice doing a particularly great job. First, tell them they did a great job, but later, write a quick note and add to their employee file. This is invaluable when you do employee reviews later.

6. Questions that employees ask you during the shift. Once you start writing down the questions, you'll be amazed at how many are repeats. At the next manager meeting, mention the repeat questions so that the other managers can address questions in shift meetings. This greatly reduces time wasted during the shift answering already answered questions freeing you to be more productive. Again, this is a proactive approach that should gain you some serious points with your GM.

Have specific goals each week that you absolutely, positively complete. Don't choose huge, magnificent goals. Small, doable goals will be great. Every restaurant has lots of projects begging to be completed that no one has time for. Examples: reorganizing or relabeling a storeroom (or both); redoing an order sheet that has been reused a million times or updating prices in your food cost database. Believe it or not, these little weekly goals add up to be significant.

Jacob League, Vice President of Operations Services, Mendocino Farms Restaurants.

Daily Organization and Reflection: Jacob calls this **First 15/ Last 15**. *He starts his day* by opening emails, then spends 15 minutes going over what he wants to accomplish that day. "At the end of my day before I leave the restaurant, I spend 15 minutes truly reflecting on the goals that I set out to do that day. If I didn't accomplish my goals, I look at what prevented me from doing that and how I will not let that happen the next day. I then write that in my book for the next day. The act of having to rewrite this is a motivation to get it done the next day".

WHAT'S THE POINT? SEEMS LIKE A LOT OF EXTRA WORK

Many new and not so new assistant managers are terrible at goal setting and time management. They think they have done a fantastic job each time they get through a shift. But the reality is they haven't done a fantastic job if they just get through a shift. Surviving a shift means accomplishing only the minimum.

Goals also work hand in hand with time management. There is always some slow time during a shift that could be productive but is usually wasted. With goals, that time can be spent to get ahead. You'll be amazed at the level of confidence this brings.

AFTER THE RUSH, GET PRODUCTIVE!

Too many managers c o a s t before the lunch or dinner shift starts, then *work like hell* during the shift, then c o a s t again when the rush is over.

It's only natural to relax after a busy shift. But rather than chatting about sports or movies or cars, spend the slow time accomplishing projects. You will help the restaurant get ahead as well as yourself. Your employees will notice, and you will probably be surprised at how they will respond to your energy.

Think about this, managers who get promoted and managers who don't get promoted spend roughly the same amount of time in the restaurant, so use your time wisely to get productive and get promoted.

DON'T BE THIS MANAGER

The rush is over. All sense of urgency has gone away. Goes into office for a while, might even sit down to have a bite to eat. Seeks out employees who are buddies and talks about sports or the weekend. When this manager sees minor infractions, like a server nibbling on food or a busser chatting with a hostess instead of bussing a table, this manager ignores them because it would interrupt what he is doing.

After the rush is over is when you should be the most proactive and focused. Start getting employees off the clock, supervising clean-up, making sure the bathrooms are clean, looking at the floors for cleanliness, and preparing for the next shift. There are a million things you could do that would keep the restaurant running efficiently, preparing for the next shift, and helping you to get out as early as possible while still doing a great job.

You will find that when you use every minute of your shift, your productivity doubles, your employees appreciate your efficiency, and you're able to leave earlier knowing that everything was done.

COMMUNICATE – ABSOLUTELY NO SURPRISES!

If, or more realistically, when you have a bad shift, such as a serious customer complaint, or one of your employees gets hurt, or anything out of the ordinary happens, make sure you document what happened and make sure you communicate to the GM what happened. No GM likes to be surprised by bad news. And never try to cover it up. Fess up, tell the GM and learn from it. First of all, telling the GM is the right thing to do and second, not telling the GM won't work. Someone will always tell the GM and then you're toast.

But be careful. Don't call your GM with unnecessary, petty questions like how much should you sell a mug to a customer. I'll never forget one GM who said to me, "Don't call me unless there is blood or flood". Good advice.

COACHING

> It is easy to point out when employees are doing something wrong. It is much better to help employees get better. There is a fine line between being a critical manager and a thoughtful, coaching manager.
>
> -ANDREW CHERNG, CEO AND FOUNDER OF PANDA EXPRESS

OBSTACLE FOR NEW RESTAURANT MANAGERS

Keep in mind that each assistant manager is responsible for his/her area. When the income statement comes out, it does not differentiate between when you were there and when you were not there. Your area is your area, every day, whether you are there or not.

Since you can't be there for all the shifts, employee training and coaching are so important.

SECURITY – A PERSONAL STORY

My daughter, Emily, was seventeen and a high school senior when she worked as a cashier at a national chain pizza restaurant. This was her first job and she had worked there for a little over 2 months. It was hard work, but she loved every minute of it.

She loved the friendships, the fast pace, and the people interaction, even the disgruntled customers.

One day, her world and the world of the restaurant's came crashing in. Four guys in jump suits and masks came through the back door. They all had pistols and screamed for everyone to get on the floor. All the employees did, but because Emily was working next to the cash register, one of the guys came over to her while she was lying down on the ground and screamed at her for the money. When she said that she didn't know where it was, the guy hit her with the pistol on the back of the head. He screamed that she was lying to him and hit her again. Then he walked over to a driver and kicked him in the ribs because he was in his way.

She came home shaking, scared, and hurt; bleeding from one of several huge bumps on the back of her head. After 2 hours in the emergency room, Emily was found not to be seriously hurt, no concussion or cracks in her skull, just a severe headache and some huge bumps.

The emergency room doctor was great: concerned, professional and caring. He said that he sees this kind of thing every night. This was not an exception. It usually doesn't make the papers, but it happens just the same. He says it's all about drugs and the cycle of drugs. Too much money in it whether you use it or not...too much money made if you sell it...too much money needed if you use it.

I was concerned that this successful robbery would give confidence to a group of bad guys that would lead to more robberies and more brutality. It was easy for them and success might encourage them to try again. But one thing is certain. The robbers came in through the back door and no security measures were being followed.

We, in the restaurant business, are guilty of being just as lax and apathetic as the typical citizen. "It's not personal and it won't happen to me". This is not true.

What would have happened if the back door had been locked? We can't know for sure, of course, the robbery might still have happened. But, then again, it might not have. Robbers usually go after the easiest victims and restaurants can be tempting targets. Restaurants have a high level of cash, few people present, many young employees and managers, and can often be careless.

Most restaurants have pretty good security systems. At least, they start out that way. In fact, Emily's restaurant had procedures that might have prevented the robbery. Always keep the back door locked and only open the door by a security password that is keyed in. They were also supposed to keep the front door locked after a certain time at night, and only open it by a button. But the procedures were not followed. No safety training was ever taught to the employees because it wouldn't be necessary; not there.

It all boils down to people and execution. Even the most sophisticated electronic systems in the world are worthless if they are not being used. They can't do what they were intended to do; protect employees.

Many restaurants use a security service to pick up deposits, have alarms for the back door, use security cameras for preventing robberies, identifying possible suspects, and have solid procedures to keep security risks at a minimum. When all systems are followed restaurants are not easy targets for robbers. They will probably move on down the road to easier pickings.

I urge restaurant managers to take security seriously; **It can happen to you**. You do not want your wife, husband, kids, parents, girlfriend, or boyfriend, to receive a phone call that you have been hurt or even killed at work. And you certainly don't want to be responsible for one of your employees getting hurt or killed that could have been prevented by you. Remember that each one of your employees is someone's daughter or son. They are not just some nameless employee.

Parents must leave the safety of their kids to you. They must trust you, just like your employees must trust you to follow procedures to keep them safe. This can be a pain to follow procedures. Your employees may not even want you to follow them because they have to chase you down when the garbage needs to go out. It takes extra work for you, too, because it's easier to just hand the backdoor keys to one of the employees or, even easier, just keep it unlocked.

THE BOTTOM LINE: EMPLOYEES ARE NOT GOING TO REMIND YOU TO FOLLOW SAFETY PROCEDURES.

They may be new, first-time employees, like Emily, who wouldn't know the first thing about safety procedures. Or they may be regular employees, even good employees. Either way, they do not fully understand the real dangers that exist if precautions are not followed.

Remember that you are the full time professional, not them. Cooks and dishwashers always want to prop open the back door to make it easier to take the trash out. Make sure you make them know that you're serious about security. Every time you start to bypass procedures and take the easy way, just think how you would feel if a robbery happened on your shift that could have been prevented by simply following procedures.

Most restaurant chains take security very seriously. In fact, you can be terminated if you don't follow security rules. Be concerned. The threat is real. It really can happen to you. Just ask Emily or me.

BE CONSISTENT

So often in my career I have seen really good assistant managers lose promotion opportunities because they got complacent and put their jobs on autopilot. They did an adequate job, but it was obvious that they were just getting through each shift, being reactive and not proactive. Don't get in the cycle of busting your butt then relaxing. Stay focused and stay sharp. It pays off.

YOUR ATTITUDE AFFECTS EVERYONE

The attitude you bring into the shift each day is crucial. You may not realize it, but your employees key off your energy, enthusiasm, and attitude. When an angry manager criticizes employees unjustly some employees internalize their anger, disappointment, or resentment but later take it out on their significant other, while you won't even remember doing it.

GOOD BOSS/BAD BOSS

Which classes do you remember from high school or college? I'll bet you don't remember the easiest classes that you had, but you probably remember the most challenging ones. Even after many years, you probably can still recall the hardest classes with the hardest teachers or professors. When they pushed you, you kicked and screamed, but you did it. You probably still remember some of the lessons that they taught. I know I can still tell you the ten foreign phrases that I had to learn in high school. I couldn't believe that we had to learn them. I mean, like, what was the use? You know what? Damned if I haven't used many of them at least once.

Interesting that the teachers and professors that pushed you and stimulated you and caused you so much grief are now looked at as some of your best, most enjoyable and rewarding periods in school. At the time, you may or may not have appreciated them, but you might now. And those easy teachers with the easy A's and no homework? I'll bet that you can't remember anything about them.

The point is that your employees today are the same as you were then. Most want to be pushed, inspired, and work at the highest level. Even if the high standards cause some temporary pain, most employees will be proud of the level of service that those standards created.

THE EASY WAY

Though it is natural for us to take the easy way if it is available and especially when it is the norm, it is equally natural for us to want to excel, to be part of "the best". When management set standards so that the only option is to perform at the highest level, along with an environment set to uphold and honor those standards, the easy way will not be an option. You'll be amazed at the transformation of your staff to bring positive peer pressure to drive your company's culture and attitudes. Productivity rises; customer satisfaction goes up, and turnover goes down. When turnover declines, sales go up and management stress goes down. All pretty good things.

All of this came out of the often-confused concept that being a "good" boss is the same as being an "easy" boss. The truth is that lenient managers are rarely confused with effective managers. Your customers and employees know the difference because they see the difference. Managers who get the reputation of being easy enjoy some short-term popularity, but they sacrifice their standards and eventually, their reputations. Effective managers enjoy long term success by keeping high standards.

EASY TRAP TO GET CAUGHT IN

One day, I had a trusted employee tell me a painful truth. It was obvious that I asked my favorite employees to do more and more while I did not ask difficult employees to do anything because I knew they would whine, gripe and resist.

If this sounds familiar, you should do something about it as soon as possible.

It's a bad habit to allow some employees to get out of doing their fair share of work. They usually do this by complaining and dragging their feet. What is really happening is that managers are allowing themselves to be "trained" by employees. The employees know that if they complain enough, some managers will find it too much trouble to ask them again. They are virtually training the managers to go to other employees who will do the extra work with no hassles or protests.

Good employees will do the work until they realize that they have been used which often results in changing a great employee into one who quits. No matter how nice, these employees eventually understand why they keep being asked to do more. I am convinced that more good employees are turned into bad employees this way than any other.

Trust me on this: your employees know who gets out of work and why. They also know which managers can be manipulated by complaining. The bottom line is good employees resent lazy employees, but they resent "weak" managers even more.

The key is to treat your employees equally. Doing this will be a hassle at first but force yourself to ask difficult employees to do things you normally would only ask your favorites to do. It is a given that some employees will resist the new you. They'll think you turned on them and are being unfair. But you will be doing the entire restaurant a great service by making it run more efficiently and fairly and you will have greatly strengthened your management skills. Morale will go up and I guarantee that you will be a far better manager.

TOO EASY OR TOO HARD?

Many new managers are confused as to whether they should be "hard" or "soft" with their employees. This is a great question that comes up with every new manager. And the answer is yes.

You need to be both hard and soft. You need both, not just one. Think of it as a tool in your toolbox. If you only had "hard" tools, what would you do when you needed a soft tool? And vice versa. You need to be able to use both.

USE THE SHIFT

When I was a general manager giving performance reviews to my assistant managers, one of the questions I would ask is what they had done to help the restaurant over the course of the review period. They would usually say "I ran good shifts, placed orders, hired, and trained employees", etc.

I said that all those things were good, but none made the restaurant better; they just kept the restaurant going status quo. To really set yourself apart from other assistant managers, wouldn't it be great if you could whip out a list of 20 projects that you had accomplished over the past 6 months?

Here's how to do that painlessly.

First step

The first step is to walk around the restaurant and make a list of all the things that need to be done. Make sure to put even the smallest projects that you see that need doing. You're not looking for big, gigantic projects that would require huge amounts of time and resources. Go deliberately to each area, each storeroom, look at order sheets, and go outside of the restaurant. You'll start to notice things that need fixing, organizing, cleaning, or updating, but no one has had the time or motivation to get them done. Here are a few examples to get you started

- Checklists that need updating or look bad
- Order lists that need updating or look bad
- Inventory prices that need updating

- Storerooms that have become disorganized with missing labels.

- Organizing the food storage or liquor storage in such a way as to speed up ordering or inventory (before you make these changes, it is a good idea to check with the GM and get the ok)

  - Minor repairs that need attention

  - Outside area that need special attention such as dumpster area

Second step

Once you've put this list together, choose which ones you want to accomplish each week. Then break those down into which day you'll accomplish each goal. Just one per week is enough. That's four per month and an impressive 24 every six months!

So, before you even start your shift you've got a specific task that you have identified to do addition to running the shift and getting through the day.

These projects are not just about you, they are about doing things that benefit the entire restaurant and management team. What this shows is that you took the initiative, identified projects that needed to be done, and got them done. This will help to make your next performance review so good that you will be looking forward to it!

DELEGATE—YOUR BEST FRIEND AND SUPERPOWER

You've got a shift to run, but you also want to accomplish your weekly tasks. What to do? A great way to do both is to delegate. Many new managers won't even consider delegating to others. They think that having someone else do the actual work somehow diminishes what they have done. They want all the credit, which means to them that they have to personally do it. But the fact is that when you delegate, you still get 100% of the credit. The best part of delegation is that you were able to run a good shift while accomplishing something else while the project or task was being done at the same time. How good is that?

SOME DOS AND DON'TS ON DELEGATING

The employee you select to delegate is important. Do NOT just grab the first employee and tell the employee this is what they are going to do. I usually chose either a really good employee who wanted some extra hours or an employee who wanted to get into management. I would also give them a free meal to sweeten the deal. Make sure you thank the employee and tell the GM how good the employee did. Win – win. You get credit for getting your project done and your employee gets the extra hours that were wanted and a meal. Be careful not to keep going to the same employee. If you ask the same employee over and over, they will tire of this no matter what incentives are offered.

Make sure you explain to the employee what you want done and that they understand. It sounds tired, but have the employee repeat back to you what it is they are going to do. This will eliminate a lot of problems. And, maybe most importantly, make sure you check back often to make sure everything is going the way you expect it to go.

WHAT WOULD YOU DO?

You are a fairly new assistant manager who is the opening manager today. You're supposed to be there at 7:00, but you arrive 30 minutes late at 7:30.

When you arrive, you find 3 prep cooks waiting for you. One of them says: "We think you should add 30 minutes to our time since we were here at 7:00. It's not our fault that we're starting late. We need the hours to pay rent."

You're really worried. Last week you were late for a closing shift and your GM was not happy but said "Just don't do it again".

You are worried about being late a second time.

What would you do?

Here's what goes through your mind:

- I'm really screwed if the GM finds out.
- Should I pay them for work they didn't do?
- Seems fair to add 30 minutes to their time.
- How do I know they were here on time?
- Do I tell the GM or not tell the GM? What if the GM finds out?
- I'm really screwed if the GM finds out.
- Do I ask the employees to not tell the GM?
- Do I pay the employees in cash out of my own pocket?
- I'm really screwed if the GM finds out.

WHAT I DID

I apologized to the cooks for being late and told them, one way or the other, I will get them their 30 minutes of pay. "My fault, not yours. I'll talk to the GM and get your pay even if I have to pay for it myself. Now, let's get to work. We've all got to work harder this morning because we're all starting late".

With this approach, your employees will be fine, respect you for accepting responsibility, and helping them get their pay. Don't worry about them not working those 30 minutes or that one or two of them might have been late themselves. Doesn't matter. You're trying to do what is right and more importantly, what your employees think is right.

I wrestled with when I should tell the GM. I hated to do it. But I sucked it up and told the GM that I had been 30 minutes late as soon as I had a few minutes. It's not good, but it is far better to be honest and upfront, than lie.

I also told the GM that I thought the employees should be compensated for the 30 minutes that they didn't work. I caused them to be late, not them. If that can't happen, I'll pay for it myself.

My GM took it about as well as I expected, which means that he did not take it well. He asked me for a plan to never be late again.

REFLECTION

Your GM will respect you for accepting responsibility and for defending your cooks. Your GM will probably agree to make up the 30 minutes administratively. There are ways to get 30 minutes added administratively, no problem. In this case, if each cook made $15 per hour, you're talking a total of $22.50. That is a small price to pay for good morale and management credibility.

If the GM hadn't agreed to add it administratively, I would have given each of them the money out of my own pocket. I told them I would so that's what you do.

The restaurant probably does not legally owe the employees, but from a "right thing to do" perspective, it is the only thing to do and is the right thing to do.

No way do you ask the cooks to keep this secret. This would destroy your integrity and on a practical note, do you really want your cooks to have this over you or be able to threaten you? Plus, you can bet that someone will tell a buddy who will tell a buddy who will tell the GM. This compromises your integrity which will be impossible to recover from. Trust is a huge part of management and you would destroy that trust. Total career suicide.

CHAPTER 3

UNDERSTANDING THE NUMBERS WILL SET YOU FREE

I hate numbers and I hate accounting.
I hate all that stuff.

I f you're like most new hospitality managers, you probably don't consider yourself a numbers person and probably (definitely) never loved taking accounting courses. The good news is that this is just another learned skill. The bad news is that it requires a little effort on your part, but, if you remember, so did learning to play the guitar. The best news is that once you understand the Profit and Loss statement (P&L), you've taken a giant step in your progress toward promotion.

In my experience the most difficult part of the P&L for new assistant managers is to get beyond the mental block that "I'm just not good at accounting". If you think you're "no good", trust me on this, you'll be no good. Plus, and this is a big plus, if you tell your GM that you're not good at something, you lose all credibility. Your GM hears you say that when something is hard, you don't want to do it. The opposite of what a promotable assistant ever says. If you're not good at something, your GM expects you to get good at it. There is no problem to admit that you're not good, but then work on it to get better. Simply making excuses why you are not good at something is never a great approach.

Once you decide to tackle the P&L, you'll be amazed that it makes sense, is logical, and isn't really all that difficult. You will see how the P&L makes the restaurant come alive and that you can influence and control your areas.

Key is realizing that the P&L is your best friend. It points out in black and white the areas you're doing good and the areas where you need to improve. The P&L is a tool for you to use so that you can excel in your job. But first, you must know and understand the P&L.

If you are serious about your career, you'll embrace the P&L (or income statement—they're the same) and not fight it. Understanding how to read and work a P&L is essential to becoming a complete manager and ready for promotion.

THE LANGUAGE OF THE P&L

The P&L has its own language that allows you to be taken seriously by your GM because you can communicate intelligently. It is like a doctor. The doctor doesn't say that you have a broken arm. The doctor says that you have a broken radius or ulna because this tells everyone which bone is broken. It's the same with the P&L. Start using the terms and they'll come naturally.

The income statement is a tool to help you perform well. It is impossible to control your areas without understanding the P&L which is essential to get promoted, rather than just talking about getting promoted. You simply cannot be successful by avoiding learning the P&L.

Your new mantra:
The P&L is my friend. The P&L is my friend

THE P&L IS YOUR REPORT CARD

You might have thought that once you got out of school, that there would be no more report cards.

Not so.

Enter the P&L. The P&L has several purposes, but the big one is this: The P&L objectively reports how well the management team is managing the restaurant. It shows if management has met budget, done worse or better than expected. But it goes further than this. Each line of the P&L is assigned to a manager and is that manager's responsibility. Since each line of the P&L has been assigned to each manager, each manager's performance can be graded individually. Basically, how you do on the P&L will play a huge role in determining who gets promoted, terminated, or passed over.

Each line on the P&L measures an expense with a budget dollar and a budget % assigned to it. Each of these lines is assigned to one manager depending upon their area of responsibility. When reading the P&L, with the exception of sales, pay closest attention to the % and not the dollars. Here's why.

The budget percentage for each line is set. The budget percentage will not change even if sales go higher than expected or lower than expected because management has set the budget based upon %'s, not $'s. As a manager, you are expected to adapt to the changes in sales. For example, when there are more sales, you can spend more dollars on food or spend more on servers. If sales go down, you are expected to use less food and use fewer servers. So, dollars will go up or down, but **percentages stay the same**.

An example:

Forecasted sales are $40,000 with expenses budgeted at 20%

Sales	expense $	expense %
$40,000	$8,000	20%

Reality happens. Actual sales trended down. If you closely monitored sales you could respond immediately by scheduling fewer and ordering less. Even though sales went down to $30,000, no problem. You hit your 20% budgeted % and you did it by spending less $. (great job!)

Sales	expense $	expense %
$30,000	$6,000	20%

If you didn't adjust your ordering or scheduling (based on sales trends), you would have kept ordering the same and scheduling the same spending $8,000 just like your budgeted $ said. Spending $8,000 when sales were only $30,000 would get you an expense % of 26.7%, or 6.7% over budget. In other words, you're in a world of hurt. In real world terms, this meant that you spent $2,000 more than you should or around $67 per day too much. The key is to monitor sales and react as soon as possible.

The next month, sales went up. You still had the same 20% expense that you needed to hit.

Sales	expense $	expense %
$45,000	$9,000	20%

When sales go up, you've got to order more food or schedule more servers to keep up. This is not a problem since with more sales, you can spend more dollars. Sales went up and even though you spent more $, you stayed at 20% (Great job!)

The key to keeping to your budget % is to know how sales are trending and responding immediately. Today. This shift. The very next employee schedule. The very next supply order.

A BIT ABOUT THE NUMBERS. WHY THE TENTH OF PERCENT IS A BIG DEAL.

At first, you may think that the percentages should be in whole numbers, not given in tenths. But here's the deal: They are given to you that way because each tenth represents a lot of money.

Let's use nice round numbers for this illustration. In this case, each month your restaurant does $100,000 in food sales and $50,000 in bar sales for $150,000 in total sales. To get a better perspective of how tenths are important, look at the table below.

$$150,000 = 100\%$$
$$15,000 = 10\%$$
$$1,500 = 1\%$$
$$150 = 0.1\%$$

Scenario 1. You are the assistant manager over servers. One of your P&L responsibilities is server labor cost. Your budget % is 5.0%, but the actual % came out to be 5.8% making you 8 tenths or 0.8% over budget. 8 tenths doesn't sound like much, but referring to the table above, it's easy to see that being over 0.8% means that you were over budget by $1,200 ($150 x 8). That sounds like a lot because it *is* a lot.

If you divide $1,200 by 30 days in a month, it means that you spent $40 too much each day. The good news is all you needed to do was save $40 per day and you would have met budget. If your servers make $10 per hour, you can see that it wouldn't take much to waste $40 per day.

The bad news is that it is easy to waste $40 per day. The keys are attention and awareness followed by action. For example, if just four servers stay on the clock for an extra 15 minutes each, there's $10 or if you have even one server who works but is not needed, yet works the entire shift, there's the entire $40. When you have 2 shifts of servers each day, it is easy to see how your payroll can quickly get out of control.

Scenario 2. You are the assistant over the bar with one of your responsibilities being bar cost. Based on bar sales of $50,000, your budget was 22.5%, but the actual cost came in as 23.2. You were over by 0.7% or $350 over budget.

50,000 = 100%
 5,000 = 10%
   500 =   1%
    50 =   0.1%

The good news: By dividing 350 into 30 days in the month, all it takes to meet budget is to save $11.66 per day.

The bad news is that it doesn't take much over pouring (or any of 1,000 other things) to waste $11.66 that would cause you to go over budget.

As you can see from the above, the sooner you react, the easier it gets to stay in budget.

FIRST, UNDERSTAND WHAT YOU'RE LOOKING AT

A basic P and L:

   Sales

   -Expenses

   = Profit or loss

Pretty simple. Subtract expenses from sales and there you go! Either a profit or a loss. When there are more sales than expenses, there's a profit. When there's more expenses than sales, there's a loss. But because sales and expenses are so broad this is zero help to a manager to control expenses. Where were sales strong or weak? Where were costs high? Who knows? It is impossible to tell, which means management could not attack the problem. But the essence of the income statement is the same as that simple one above. The only difference is that your income statement is more detailed because the purpose is to help management.

So, let's look at an example of a typical unit income statement. Remember, the income statement is our report card that measures management's performance, but it also helps management locate problem areas so that we can look good. To do that, sales and costs must give management enough information to find what is over or under budget. The income statement does this by splitting up each area of sales and expenses into many sub areas. Except for sales, the % is more important than $.

SALES OR "TOPLINE"

Sales can be split up in many ways depending upon which ones management considers the most important. Here's one example.

Sales	$	%
Food sales		
Lunch		
Dinner		
Take out		
Total food sales		
Beverage sales		
Liquor		
Beer		
Wine		
Total Beverage sales		
Total Food and Beverage Sales		

Sales are from food, beverages, t-shirts, whatever. Sales never include sales tax because you only collect taxes; you don't own it and you can't spend it, so it's not included in sales. **Total** sales % is always 100%. What you're looking for is comparisons and trends. For example, if you had a contest to sell more wine, having wine sales separated, helps you determine if wine sales went up compared to last month.

The **cost of sales** is where it gets interesting. This is one of the most important costs that can make or break a restaurant. Cost of sales are the dollars that it cost to make whatever it is the company makes. It includes **only** the actual costs to make the product, not even labor is included. For a car manufacturer, this would include the engine, wheels, transmission, etc. In restaurants, our products are food and beverages. If you can't eat it or drink it, it's not included in the cost of sales.

Food costs can be broken down in many ways, depending upon what is most important to your type of restaurant. For example, if you had a sports bar, you might break out chicken wings from food because wings are so important to the food cost. Note that beverage is restaurant speak for anything alcoholic; beverages never include nonalcoholic beverages, such as tea, coffee, lemonade, etc. Non-alcoholic beverages are included with food. Only when it says total cost of sales, does it include both food and beverages.

Food costs and beverage costs are broken down (categorized) so that management can find where a problem is if a cost is over budget. The categories vary tremendously between restaurant chains. Below is a typical breakdown. Since each category has a budget % assigned to it, it is easy to see when you are over or under budget. However, knowing *where* a problem is does not tell you how to *fix* a problem and fixing the problem is why you're paid the big bucks. Variance just means difference.

FOOD COST OF SALES

	Actual %	Budget %	Variance %
Meat	11.2%	10.1	1.1 over
Seafood	9.2	8.9	0.3 over
Produce	2.9	3.0	0.1 over
Bread	1.3	1.2	0.1 over
Dairy	2.1	1.2	0.9 over
Other	2.0	2.1	0.1 under
Total food cost of sales	28.7	26.5	2.6 over

Having the problem located as specifically as possible helps management locate where the problem is. That's why Food costs and Beverage costs are broken down even more. In the example above, you're over 2.6%. It looks like the major problem areas were meat (over 1.1%) and dairy (over 0.9) because just these two areas were where 2% of the 2.6% were over.

FOOD COST (AND ALCOHOL COST) ARE DIFFERENT

Some managers think they can lower food cost by spending less on food. This is not even a little bit true. That kind of thinking is also why some restaurants run out of menu items on the last day of the month.

It does *seem* to make sense that spending less on food should result in lower food costs since it works that way with supplies. So why not food and beverage costs?

The reason is that food cost is figured differently than the cost of supplies. The cost of supplies is simple and straight forward. So, if sales go up, buy more supplies to keep the same percentage. When sales go down, buy less supplies. Then divide the total supply cost into total sales and Bang! Supply cost %. Simple.

Food cost, though, is a little more complicated. The good news is that it does make sense. The biggest difference is that you don't just add up all of the food invoices and then divide into sales, like supplies.

The reason that food and beverage cost is different than supplies is that food costs use only the money spent on food (or beverages) that went to produce sales to customers. Since food cost is only about the food spent to generate customer spending, it means that the money spent on food that is still on your shelves at the end of the month does not count and any money spent for discounted meals for employees and managers or for comping customers do not count either. Only the money spent on customers.

There's a formula to figure this out. Wait! Don't turn away. It's not too bad. It even makes sense, so give it a chance.

The formula is:

BI (beginning inventory) + food purchases – EI (ending inventory) = food cost of sales

BI is the amount of money spent on food that was on your shelves at the beginning of the month. To get the real, honest, and actual cost, first get the amount of money that was tied up on your shelves at the beginning of the month (BI), then add in all the food invoices during the month. So, you've got the total amount that you started with (BI) plus the invoices of expenses that you bought during the month. This gives the entire amount of food that could have been used for customers. But it also includes food that **could** have been stolen, lost, thrown away, over portioned, spoiled, wasted, discounted to managers and employees, and food that was not delivered, but still charged for.

Any food that is still on your shelves at the end of the month is simply not counted in the month's food cost. The food on the shelves (or the walk-in, freezer, tables, cabinets) are counted and added up making the ending inventory or EI.

This amount (EI) is subtracted from the total of BI + Purchases. Since the EI is still on your shelves and walk-in, it doesn't matter if you get a truckload of food delivered on the last day of the month. It has no effect on food cost. That's why there is no reason to run out of food because you're trying to decrease food cost. Just doesn't work that way.

After this, the only thing left to do is to subtract employee and manager discounts and comps (such as meals to customers that weren't charged for over cooked food) to give a pure food cost of sales. These are subtracted from cost of sales, so managers are not penalized for giving employees the benefit of discounted food.

Discounted meals are a common benefit for employees and managers. Most restaurants give employees who are working meals for free or discounted. If this food were counted in the food cost, it would raise food costs which would definitely discourage managers from   giving discounts. But, because these discounts do not affect food cost, managers can give this benefit and not have hungry employees or managers.

GREAT. I KNOW WHERE THE PROBLEM IS, BUT WHAT DO I DO?

Referring back to the food cost table, Dairy is 0.9 high. The first step might be to go into the walk-in to see if there is out-of-date milk, sour cream, etc. Ask the prep cooks if they have thrown away any milk (or other dairy products). Be careful how you ask this, you want them to answer honestly, not blame them for anything, you're just trying to find out if the order level is set too high.

If you see old dates, then it means that you are over ordering and probably means your prep cooks have been throwing away old product. The solution would be to redo your par levels ASAP. Also tell your prep cooks to let you know when you've got anything out of date. They want to help, but you've got to let them know you want their help. It would also be worth checking the portion sizes that are being served. Do the math: over portioning just one ounce per customer adds up when there are hundreds of customers per shift, 2 shifts per day, and 60 shifts per month.

If meat cost is high, there are several things to check:

1. Since meats are very expensive relative to most other foods, the first action is to check the dates to see if any cases are close to spoiling. If so, you're ordering too much, and some could have been thrown away.

2. Make sure (really sure) that each time you get a delivery someone checks the meat delivery all the way into the walk-in. If the invoice says three cases of strip steaks, make sure there are 3 cases of strip steaks.

NOTE: The delivery guy knows which managers do a good job checking deliveries and which ones do not. Eventually, you'll be shorted a case of meat. BANG. High food cost.

Some managers just check how many total cases are on the invoice, then count to make sure the same number of cases are delivered. Ordered 12 cases, received 12 cases. Perfect. But, not so quick. This is not good enough because all meats are not created equal meaning they don't all cost the same. Invariably, the expensive case of meat will be missing, but a cheaper case of meat will be there. Be careful. The drivers know which managers just count cases.

3. The next check is to see if you have been ripped off. If one of your cooks decided to take even one steak per shift, your meat cost would be sky high by the end of the month. To put a quick stop to this, count the number of steaks at the beginning of each shift, subtract out the steaks sold during the shift, then count again at the end of each shift. The number of steaks remaining should equal the number of steaks you started with minus the steaks sold. Do this at the beginning and end of each shift and you will not have more theft, if that was the problem. Once you do it a couple of times, this becomes routine, not taking much time at all.

4. Check the invoices that were used to figure out the monthly food expenses. Someone could easily have written the wrong number.

5. Lock the walk-in whenever it is not used for long periods of time like between shifts and at night.

6. Restrict who can go into the walk-in. No servers, for instance.

COMMUNICATE THE PROBLEM – DON'T JUST CARRY IT AROUND

Whenever you have a food cost problem, it is very (very!) important to tell your cooks. Or tell your bartenders when you have an alcohol cost problem. Don't accuse, just tell them because you want their help. Telling them helps in two ways. The first lets everyone know that you are aware that meat cost is high. If one of the cooks is actually stealing steaks, they will probably stop when they realize you know there is a problem. The second reason is to get the cooks to help. But they can't help if they don't know there's a problem! You would be surprised at how often they solve the problem. Getting them involved is key.

Important: A common rookie mistake when figuring the cost % is to divide food cost into total sales (food and alcohol), instead of only food sales. Likewise, to get an accurate wine cost, wine cost is divided into wine sales, NOT total alcohol sales, and definitely not total sales. The same is true for beer and liquor. To get accurate beer cost, divide beer cost into beer sales and to get an accurate liquor cost, divide liquor cost into liquor sales. Basically, just remember, apples to apples and you'll be ok.

Gross Profit is total sales minus total cost of sales. The only expense that has been subtracted from total sales is the total cost of sales (the cost of both food and beverages). The only way to have a higher gross profit % is to have your customers pay more (higher check average) or for you to pay less on cost of sales.

Operating expenses (sometimes called controllable expenses because every expense can be controlled by unit management) are the expenses that relate to running or operating the restaurant. These expenses *are* affected by sales, and why they're also called variable expenses, because the dollars vary with sales. The more sales you have, the more it costs. For example, if you normally have 7 servers at lunch, but sales increase, you need to add another server. If sales go down, you reduce the number of servers.

Operating expenses include employee and management labor, utilities (gas, electricity, water, and internet), supplies (bar, kitchen, dining room, and cleaning), repairs and maintenance. Operating expenses include all expenses (besides cost of sales) that unit management is responsible for.

LABOR COST IS THE BIG KAHUNA IN OPERATING EXPENSES

That and cost of sales are usually the two largest (thus most important) expenses to control. Labor cost can be influenced by many factors, such as scheduling, payrates, overtime, and training.

I personally think that scheduling is the most important factor. Be very careful when doing your scheduling. When you post a schedule, you are approving payroll checks, affecting your employee's income, and going a long way in meeting or not meeting your labor budget.

Before posting, check past sales and future events, such as the number of reservations you have, banquets scheduled, and any events that may be going on near your restaurant that affect sales, like road closures or movie openings. It is best to develop a system to determine how many servers (or hosts, cooks, etc.) are needed. One way is to look at forecasted sales. For instance, for every $400 in sales forecasted, one server is added.

I remember when I had just gotten promoted to assistant manager, I was put in charge of servers and did my first server schedule. Later, I had worked the opening shift and got home around 6pm. I had just sat down to dinner with my wife when I got a call from my GM who was working the close shift. He said to get back in now.

"Now, I said?" "NOW", he said. "OK", I said.

The GM told me there were way too many servers and they were unhappy. I needed to get my ass back to sort it out. Being very quick, I caught on that the GM was not happy with me. At the time, I lived in Houston, Texas and was about 40 minutes away from the restaurant. It was now rush hour, so make that an hour to the restaurant. Fun. Not.

When I got there, I could see what he meant. There were far too many servers. I sorted the servers out by asking who wanted to leave. I redid the server schedule that night and reposted the schedule after spending a lot of time reviewing past sales numbers for each day of the week and looking ahead to future events. Serious lesson learned.

I still vividly remember this incident and although it was a pain at the time, the GM was right to have me fix the problem. This really drove home to me how important scheduling is. Bad scheduling can totally screw up shifts and disrupts employees but is also the key ingredient that makes or breaks your labor cost.

As a sidenote, in the US when a shift is slow, managers can ask employees to go home without paying them. In several European countries, Finland for one, once you post a schedule, management is obligated to pay for the entire shift, whether they go home or not.

Moving on to repairs and maintenance. This is often grouped together as R & M, but each is different. Repairs cover unexpected expenses (like a broken window) while Maintenance includes scheduled tasks that are performed on a regular basis, such as carpet cleaning, window washing, hood vent cleaning, lawn mowing, and others.

Operating income (sometimes called controllable income). Gross profit minus Operating expenses = Operating income. This is an important category because this is where many management bonuses are figured. This makes sense since all the expenses above are completely and totally in management's control.

Fixed expenses are expenses that are NOT affected by sales, such as rent, insurance, interest, and depreciation and that management has no control of, at least not at the unit level. Fixed expenses stay the same dollar amount each month regardless if sales go up or down. This is one reason why fixed expenses are usually given in dollars (rather than %) because their actual dollar amount is known (and doesn't change). Unit managers don't usually pay much attention to this since they can't control them and fixed expenses usually don't affect their bonus. Upper management gets to worry about this.

SO HOW DO I READ A P&L? WHAT AM I LOOKING FOR?

Take it in steps: get a notepad and a quiet spot.

Step one: Your P&L will probably have $ and % for current month, last month, quarter, and Year to Date (YTD). First step is to highlight your areas of responsibility. For example, if servers are your area of responsibility, highlight server labor, dining room supplies, and any other areas of responsibility.

Step two: Scan your highlighted areas of the current month. You are looking for any %'s that are over or under 0.5% of budget. If there are any, these are your primary problem areas.

Step three: Identify any areas that are over budget, but less than 0.5%.

Step four: Your job now is to think about why each area over 0.5% was over budget. Look at overtime and training. Are they high? Is either one responsible for Did you have a lot of turnover last month causing to hire and train more than normal? High turnover causes a lot of training, which in turn can cause OT because some servers had to work more than normal.

Step five: Now that you know why you were over budget by 0.5% or over, you can develop a plan for each area that will lower the $ so that the percentage is within budget for the month that you are in now. Remember, you are concerned with the percentage. The dollars will vary depending upon sales, so make sure you take into account how sales are going this month.

THE P&L IS NOT FAIR.

Let's say your restaurant is open for lunch and dinner seven days a week. So, 7 days a week times lunch and dinner shifts equal 14 shifts.

But wait!

You work only 5 shifts! You are not there for 9 out of 14 shifts. Yet, when the P&L comes out at the end of the month, you're totally responsible for your area even when you haven't been there most of the time. How can that be?

It be.

You are responsible for your area whether you are there or not there.

Because you can't be there for every shift, you must rely on and trust your employees. That's why effective employee training and getting your employees to buy into your goals on a personal level are so important.

Sometimes the best indicator of how good a job you're doing is when you're not there. If you feel you must be at work to make sure your employees are doing a good job, then you're doing something wrong.

When managers tell me that they had to work 60-80 hours to ensure their employees were doing a good job, I know there is a problem, and the problem is almost always with the manager. A vicious cycle can start when the manager is over budget. The manager believes the answer is to put in more and more hours which can lead to performance going down further because they're exhausted. Then add in feeling guilty for neglecting family and friends and frustration because of the long hours and come to the wrong conclusion that all the effort and sacrifice should be worth something.

Obviously, this is a recipe for disaster as the manager works long hours, resentment builds, his family suffers, and performance declines. Often, all the hours spent leads to no improvement. Very frustrating. Very stressful.

Let's get something out of the way here. While effort is good, effort without results is not good and means nothing. So, get rid of the idea that working long hours will help excuse bad performance. It won't.

The answer is to figure out what the problem is. Either your employees have not been trained correctly, gotten into bad or lazy habits because they weren't consistently coached, internal or external theft is happening, or you're just paranoid and you should not work so much. All of which are on you.

> **WARNING:**
>
> No matter how bad the pressure to do better on the P&L gets, do not be tempted to cheat!
>
> It is not worth your career, your reputation, and having to tell your significant other why you have been fired.
>
> Find the problem and fix it.

The answer is to find the problem and solve it. If you just cover it up, the problem still exists, and you'll just have to cover it up even more next month. Eventually, you'll get caught. When you first see a problem, fix it. If you don't know how to solve the problem, get help. There is no shame in asking for help. Every manager has occasional P&L problems. Get help.

Getting help is smart management, not weak management. If you're in a chain, find which restaurants are doing especially well in your problem areas, and visit, email, or call them to find out what they do differently or what they recommend. They'll be glad to help.

SOME P&L BASICS

At its most basic, the dollars and percentages of a P&L is like a funnel with sales going into the top, expenses subtracted, and if there are more sales than expenses a profit comes out the bottom. Sales taxes are never included in sales because, unfortunately, sales taxes are not yours. The restaurant only collects sales taxes for state and local governments.

Sales, revenue, and top line all mean the same thing. Income on the other hand means profit, so never call revenue income or income revenue.

If the P&L only gave you sales and expenses, it would be no help at all because sales and expenses are just too broad to be able to pinpoint a problem. You'd have no idea where your sales came from (lunch or dinner, food, or alcohol, etc.) or which expenses were high (meat or produce, busser or server labor, kitchen supplies or dining rooms supplies). Meaning of course, that you would have a tough time knowing where problems were and more importantly, where to start fixing them. Which leads into the next subject where did the budget numbers come from?

THE BUDGET NUMBERS

The budget dollars and percentages are based on how upper management want to run the business – the level of customer service (do servers have 3 or 4 table stations?), the quality of the food and beverage desired and required (does it require organic?), and what level of maintenance and cleanliness is acceptable.

TOP LINE AND BOTTOM LINE

Sales (or revenue) are at the top of the P&L, so it is often called the top line. Income, on the other hand, usually means profit. After all the expenses have been paid, at the bottom of the P&L is net income or the bottom line.

WHY BEING UNDER BUDGET CAN BE AS BAD AS BEING OVER BUDGET

If the server and hostess labor cost was way under budget, it might mean that the dining room manager cut costs by scheduling fewer servers to cover the same amount of tables or scheduled one fewer host that was required. That would be cutting customer service by not having the staffing required. Being under budget will catch this.

OK, OK. I GET IT. THE P&L IS IMPORTANT. NOW WHAT?

The first order of business is to make sure that you know which lines on the P&L you are personally responsible for and two, the budget for each line. If you are not sure, suck it up, and ask your general manager. You've got to know, don't assume you know. You've got to know what's on the test!

For example, let's say you are in charge of the beverage (bar) department. Your P&L responsibilities typically include the cost of sales for liquor, beer, and wine; bar supplies expense; bartender, bar servers, and bar back labor expenses, including overtime and training expenses and possibly uniform expense.

Of course, you are also responsible for employee morale, cleanliness, quality of training, customer service and your ability to manage on your shifts, but we're just covering the P&L right now.

Next, what is the budget for each of your areas? It will be right on the P&L. Get the past several months' worth of P&L's. Compare them from month to month. Are they getting worse, better, staying the same? Is there one area in particular that is regularly high? Use a highlighter and look for the consistent problem areas. Which areas did the previous manager do well and not so well? How much over or under budget has your lines of responsibility been?

Make note of the areas that are way over budget, just a little over, meeting budget, and which ones are under budget.

Start with the premise that anything within 1/2% of budget is OK, but any more or less than that is too much over (or under) budget. In other words, if you have a labor budget of 3.2%, you'll want to be within 2.7 - 3.7%. But check with your GM to see where the range should be.

IMPORTANT STEP

Once you know which lines of responsibilities on the P&L

are yours, then determine which ones look good and which ones need work. Unfortunately, just knowing where you are over budget doesn't tell you what to do. The real work, of course, lies in knowing what the numbers mean and being able to translate the numbers into actions to correct the problems.

THE BIG QUESTION

The big question: do you know WHY your numbers are above or below budget?

When I was GM, I required each assistant manager to explain why any line of their responsibility was over or under by ½% or more. The reason is that if they knew why they were over or under, I wasn't too worried, because I knew they could fix it. If they had no idea why, I knew they couldn't fix it and knew they were not in control of their areas.

If you know why, it means you are in control! If you don't know why, it means that each of your areas could get better or worse, but not because of you. Things just happen. In other words, you have no idea why you are over (or under) budget, but worse, if you don't know why, you have no idea how to fix it.

If you don't know why, then you are admitting that you have no idea what happened. You can't take credit if it was good, but you can and will have full responsibility if it was bad.

But the worst part, the most damning part is that you really aren't managing effectively. You were not in control. It was just luck (bad or good) that you got what you got.

This is not the way for promotion. You've got to make your P&L's deliberate.

INSTANT GRATIFICATION

One of the typical traits of hospitality managers is that we like instant gratification. The beauty of hospitality P&L's is that they respond almost instantly to your actions and you can track them daily. So, when you start to do things to help, you'll be able to see if they helped almost immediately.

SO, WHAT TO DO? WHAT TO DO?

The real work, of course, lies in knowing what the numbers mean and then translating the numbers into actions that enables you to meet budget.

Several things to do, so let's get to it.

> *Don't wait till the official P&L comes out: Know as soon as possible by monitoring costs during the month.*

The corporate P&L usually comes out in the first part of the following month, usually between the 3rd and the 10th of the month. The problem with waiting 3 to 10 days to find out how you're doing is that when there is a problem, (such as over-portioning, or theft, or any of a million other things), the problem is going on each day. If you totally rely on the P&L to find out where you are high, those first 3 days have already done damage to your month. You're already behind!

The remedy is to know as soon as possible, way before the P&L comes out. You can do this by creating your own mini P&L that monitors costs during the month. You and your GM don't want to be surprised when the P&L comes out. P&L surprises mean that you are not in control of your area.

The good news is that a P&L can be controlled. In fact, you can have great control over it leaving very little, if anything, to chance. Even waiting 3 days is way too long to find out, much less starting to do something about it. The longer you wait, the more difficult it is to fix.

Note: Just because your GM or other assistant managers are not doing this, does not mean you can't. You can and you should.

So, here's how to do it

Here's one way to get you in control of your P&L areas and establish yourself as someone promotable. This works for almost anything, labor, bar cost, etc., but is particularly useful for supplies. Just log the numbers each day in Excel or, if you're old school, on paper.

First step: The example below works for any type of supplies. The daily supplies column comes from the invoices of supplies that have come in. With this simple form, you can know exactly how much you are spending on your area of supplies and the percentage that you'll have at the end of the month.

Date	Supplies $ daily	Supplies $ MTD	Sales $ daily	Sales $ MTD	Daily %	MTD %
Oct 1	75	75	5,000	5,000	1.5	1.5
Oct 2	0	75	5,500	10,500	00	.71
Oct 3	200	350	7,500	18,000	2.7	1.9

Don't pay attention to Month to Date (MTD) %'s during the first 10 days or so because the %'s will go way up and way down. But, by the 15th day or so, it will begin to give you pretty close to an accurate % of what you'll wind up with at the end of the month.

• If the trend shows going over budget, reduce your spending by only ordering what is essential to make it until the end of the month.

• If it is showing your % as below, go ahead and spend more on supplies to get it just below budget. You'll still be within budget this month and you'll be in really great shape next month, since you'll have less to order. You won't have to order as much so that you are almost guaranteed to be under budget.

You are striving to always be at or under budget each and every month. The above procedure allows you to be in control of your areas. If you must go over budget, you will at least know why. Remember, when you know why, you're in control and can fix any problem.

> **WARNING:**
>
> Do not run out of anything essential!
> It is better to go over budget than to run out!

One time when I was in charge of the servers, I was over budget with dining room supplies. After looking into it, I noticed that each month I ordered dozens of forks, knives and spoons. I suspected the bussers were carelessly throwing the silverware away when they were back in the kitchen. So, to test this, one dinner shift, I brought in a child's blow up wading pool, probably 3 feet wide and plopped it down in part of the kitchen. As a busser came in with a loaded bus tub, I stopped him and told him to dump the entire contents of the bus tub into the little wading pool. I told each busser that if there was no silverware, I would clean it up myself and I would give him $50 on the spot. I did this again a week later and gladly paid each busser $50. Because everyone was aware of the problem, the problem sorted itself out.

This proactive approach has two advantages over waiting till the official P&L comes out. The obvious one is to know and be able to adjust as the month goes along. If it looks like you're going to go over budget, cut way down on your purchases, only buying the necessities. Don't just order what some par stock says.

The second advantage is that when you do get the official P&L, compare your logged invoices with the invoices that corporate charged to your department. They should be equal. If they're not, either you or the corporate office input an invoice into the wrong department. This also has the added benefit of making sure you have all the invoices. You may be surprised at invoices that you missed or added. The corporate office doesn't usually make input mistakes, but it does happen. You don't want to look bad just because there was an accounting error.

Second step: For each area over budget, identify and list every single way you could be over budget. For bar costs for instance, this would include

Bartenders: over pouring; pouring beer after beer trying to get rid of beer foam; giving drinks away; not ringing up drinks; theft of beer, wine, or liquor.

Suppliers: missing bottles from your beer, liquor, or wine deliveries.

Admin: invoices not correct, either you have logged them incorrectly or the home office has. Double check all invoices that are listed as expenses compared to what you have.

Third step: For each of the possible problems from above, make procedures or actions that you could implement that would correct them. For example, for over pouring, always require a jigger be used. For wasting beer because of beer foam, instruct your bartenders to alert you or the manager on duty that there is a problem with the beer pressure or keg. Don't just keep wasting beer. For potential missing bottles from deliveries, make sure each manager goes with the delivery guy into the restaurant and ensures the order. Never just sign the invoice without checking the delivery.

Fourth step: Get the members of your team to buy in. One of the problems that many assistants have (and some GM's) is to carry the monkey of responsibility on your shoulders without letting your employees know that there are problems. Let them know! You want each member of your team to understand that your costs are high, and you are going to address the problem. Often, just by letting them know that you know the costs are high, your costs will go down when your employees know you are paying close attention and care.

HIGH LABOR COST

One of the biggest challenges facing restaurant managers is how to lower their labor cost when it is high. More specifically, where do you start to look for the cause of the problem?

Here's how to do it

This technique works the same for any position, but for this example, let's say you are responsible for the servers.

First step is to figure out how much your schedule is costing. Do this for each shift, such as Monday Lunch, Monday Dinner, Tuesday lunch, Tuesday dinner, etc. It is a little tedious to first setup, but with the help of Excel, a few formulas, and copy and paste, not too bad.

Here's an example:

Monday lunch

	Scheduled in	Scheduled out	Hours worked	Hourly rate	Amount paid
1st server	10:00	2:00	4.0	$10.00	$40.00
2nd server	10:30	2:00	3.5	$10.00	$35.00
3rd server	11:00	2:30	3.5	$10.00	$35.00
4th server	11:15	3:00	3.7	$10.00	$37.00
5th server	11:30	4:00	4.5	$10.00	$45.00
		Total hours worked	19.2	Total paid	$192.00

Monday dinner

	Scheduled in	Scheduled out	Hours worked	Hourly rate	Amount paid
1st server	4:00	9:00	5.0	$10.00	$50.00
2nd server	4:30	9:00	4.5	$10.00	$45.00
3rd server	5:00	10:00	5.5	$10.00	$55.00
4th server	5:15	10:30	5.2	$10.00	$52.00
5th server	5:30	11:00	5.5	$10.00	$55.00
	Total hours worked		25.7	Total paid	$257.00

Grand total hours worked Monday 44.9

Grand total wages paid Monday $449.00 ($192 + $257)

Do this for each shift for all 7 days in the week. If your employees are paid every two weeks, just double the week's hours worked to the dollars spent to get the total hours and total dollars for the payroll period.

Then when the actual payroll comes out, compare the scheduled server in and out times with the actual in and out times. You will immediately see where you are over. You might have forgotten that you had to add a server or that there was overtime.

The employee schedule that you write is a big deal. You are essentially controlling people's lives, approving how much they make, and how much your restaurant spends. In many countries, once you've made the schedule, the schedule is locked in, with management required to pay employees for the entire time that is scheduled, regardless if you send them home. Here in the US, schedules are much more forgiving as we can just get people to clock out.

Rule one. Know as soon as possible when any of your areas are a problem. Each day you delay, the problem continues and multiplies. If bartenders or cooks are over portioning $10 a day, that's $300 per month that you will be over. And that is just one area.

A FEW SOLUTIONS TO COMMON PROBLEMS

If you find yourself with a persistent P&L problem, do not be tempted to cheat. As a manager, you'll have many opportunities to do this, from taking cash to padding inventories. Resist! Your integrity, your reputation, and your career are not worth the short-term gain. If you have a cost problem, admit you have a cost problem, seek solutions, and then fix it, rather than obscure the problem. The problem will only get worse.

How can I (easily) figure out how to price a special (or anything)?

Q – I've got a left-over meat that costs $4. What should the price be if I need a 29% food cost?
First step – find the multiple
Use this formula 1 / desired cost %
I want a 29% cost.
1 / 0.29 = 3.4 This is the multiple
Second step – multiply cost x multiple
3.4 x $4 = $13.60
This shows that if you charge $13.60, the food cost will be 29%.
But then look at the price and value. You might want to price it higher or lower depending on your restaurant's pricing or how badly you want to sell the product. But the important point here is that you will know the cost and you are not guessing.

WHAT DO I DO WHEN MY COSTS ARE HIGH?

Get your employees involved

Like I stated earlier, let your employees know there is a problem. Get the members of your team to buy in to the problem. One of the problems that many assistants have is to carry all the responsibility on their shoulders when there is a problem. When you carry this burden by yourself, you'll start to resent your employees for not caring and develop a bad attitude because you'll think you're the only one troubled by the high costs (and you would be right, but no one else knows).

Trust your employees

They really will care, but you've got to give them a reason to care by letting them know that there is a problem first. Let them know which costs are high. This serves two purposes: 1) your employees will now be aware, and I'll bet they suggest ways to help or at the very least will be more careful.

Should I allow my bartenders to recognize new or regular customers by giving free drinks away?

Yes and no. I know this is counter intuitive but here's my experience. I first allowed each bartender to give away 3 shift drinks to recognize regular customers. And they did. They gave away 3 drinks each shift. This quickly got out of hand and was way too expensive.

I then took away the 3-drink limit but said that I still wanted them to be able to recognize regular bar customers, but there was no limit. The bartenders were stunned, they just knew I was going to take this privilege away, not give them even more freedom. But, interestingly, each shift they gave away between zero and 2 drinks, never 3 and only occasionally 2. I believe that they felt empowered and trusted. They knew I could take this away at any time and they did not want to lose the privilege.

WHAT WOULD YOU DO?

You are a manager in a chain with multiple units in a city. A couple of weeks ago you hired a server from another company restaurant nearby who said the reason he left was that he hadn't been getting enough shifts. After a couple of weeks, you got a call from one of the managers of the other restaurant that he used to work for. They had heard he was working there and that they wanted to let you know that he was terminated for being constantly late, not showing up for shifts.

If you got this call, what would you do?

WHAT YOU *COULD* DO:

- Could fire him for lying.
- Could just say thanks to the manager who called and do nothing.
- Could talk to the employee and ask him to explain himself.
- Could tell the employee that you know what really happened and that he had better be careful.

WHAT I DID

On the next shift that the server worked, I immediately confronted him. I was aggressive with him and told him I had just got off the phone with the other restaurant and knew why he'd really quit. That I was disappointed in him for lying and that he better watch it. The server quit just a few days after I had confronted him.

REFLECTION

I think I screwed up. Today, I would thank the manager for calling and letting me know, but I would do nothing. Now, I believe that letting the server start over again would be best. I would keep his past information to myself. But the first time the server called off or was late, I would pull him aside and privately let him know that I know what happened and that I hope this wasn't starting again. I think he would get the point.

There are three kinds of accountants:
those that can count and those that can't

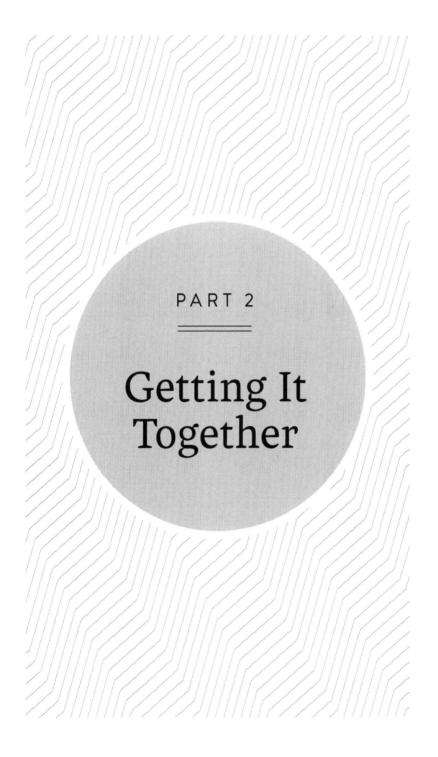

PART 2

Getting It Together

CHAPTER 4

EMPLOYEES

Don't lose a good one,
don't keep a bad one

How important are your employees? Simple. Your success depends upon them. When you first arrive as the new assistant manager, you're going to be nervous. But your employees are just as nervous about you. Each employee knows they will have to re-establish themselves with the "new guy". They're going to have to start from zero with you after they had already "broken in" the last assistant manager. They knew what they could and couldn't do, but now they don't know what to expect from you.

As an assistant manager, you will be over one department that will be yours and yours only, except of course, when you're shift manager, you'll also be over the entire restaurant. So, as you get to know your employees, make your expectations clear, your standards known, and what you're about.

YOU CREATE THE ENVIRONMENT

Establishing an environment is a top-down process, but what if you´re the 'down' in the top-down process? Do you have any influence in the environment?

The answer is yes. You play a huge part in ensuring that employees have an environment where they feel secure and can flourish as individuals yet have the highest customer service standards.

You're not the GM, but you can still make a huge difference. Even if you have the world's biggest jerk as a GM, you can help by treating each employee as important and creating an environment that is supportive, at least while you're there. By doing that your employees will be able to bounce back from even the worst day.

Here are points to consider to help create that supportive environment:

Know your employees. Each employee works for a different reason, whether for advancement, to pay the bills, or some other reason. Know what they are.

Have consistent moods. Even if you are a jerk, at least be a jerk every day. Good guy one day, bad guy the next day type of management only confuses everyone.

Be consistent in rules and structure. Even the tightest rules are tolerable if they are consistently enforced.

Analyze your rules. Are there any that don't make sense? Are there some that even management hates to enforce? Identify and eliminate those or at least come to some kind of compromise. This will not be seen as a sign of weakness, but as a strength.

Honor work schedules. Don't try to force your part time employees to be full time employees. You may succeed in coercing them to work in the short term, but you risk losing them permanently or damaging a great attitude. Just not worth the risk.

Your employees want to do well. They didn't start to work by expecting anything less than success.

FIRST PRIORITY

Your first priority is to get to know your employees so that you know who you can trust, who you can depend on, who is strong, who is weak, who the informal leaders are, and who the slackers are. One very important tool is to be an active listener. This means when you ask questions you listen to what they say rather than think about what you are going to say while they are talking. This shows that you are truly interested in them, rather than just checking the box that you talked to your employees. Believe it or not, you will probably learn something. Listening takes time but is worth it.

> **CAUTION:** Be wary of first impressions; give yourself time before you start to think you know the employees. That one employee you thought was a superstar? A little later you may realize that this employee was actually a slacker who was just good at sucking up.

ATTITUDE

Your attitude may not be the asset that makes you a great leader, but without a great attitude, you won't go far. It is sometimes tough to keep a great attitude at work, but it is absolutely necessary. The effect of a leader's attitude on others is remarkable. When you show up with a bad attitude, employees feel it instantly, will avoid you if possible, and worse, their attitude goes down too. It is important to take responsibility for your attitude. Whatever happens at home or anywhere else, don't let it prevent you from having a positive attitude at work. You don't want to get the reputation of being moody by letting your personal life interfere with work.

KNOW YOUR EMPLOYEES

*"We are not as good as we think we are,
and others are not as bad as we think they are."*

-ANDREW CHERNG, CEO PANDA EXPRESS

Remember they are individuals first, with their own goals, motivations, and reasons for being at work. Some managers forget that and think of them only as "the help", getting to know their employees just enough to know their names. That isn't enough. Dig deeper to find out why each employee is working at your restaurant.

This is super important, because once you know why, you can understand their motivations. Once you know why they're working, you'll be able to help them succeed even if it means that they will eventually leave. Besides being fair and consistent, helping them to achieve their goals is the best thing you can do to get employees to trust you and build loyalty.

WHAT YOUR EMPLOYEES WANT VS WHAT MANAGERS *THINK* EMPLOYEES WANT

There's an interesting study that asked employees what they wanted most from their jobs. They also asked managers what *they* thought employees wanted most from their jobs.

Managers answered that they thought that employees most cared about money. Employees answered that they most cared about feeling appreciated for the work they do.

There is a disconnect here that makes motivating your employees so much tougher than it has to be. Having managers think that money is the prime motivator for employees when the reality is just showing appreciation can only lead to bad morale and frustration for both managers and employees. Showing that you care costs nothing and motivates your employees to continue to do a great job. Sounds like a win-win to me. I mean who doesn't like an "attaboy"? Managers who continue to use money as a power play limits their ability to manage effectively.

What do your employees need to be successful?

Your employees will get a great first impression of you when you come in humble, ask questions of everyone, and care about the job. When your employees realize that you respect them and the jobs they do, they'll tend to do their job the right way, even when you're not there because they feel loyal to you. Some examples:

- For the single parent with kids to support, one very big priority is usually a steady, regular schedule so they can plan for daycare, school pick-ups, shopping, etc.

- For college students working their way through college or high school, honor their part time schedules.

- For the employee who wants to get into management, get them opportunities to distinguish themselves by delegating projects or cross training. Get them noticed.

- For the employee who is obviously working with English as a second language, explore nearby ESL courses. Usually, these courses are free or have a nominal price which the restaurant could pick up along with transportation. This can lead the employee to advance to better paying jobs in your restaurant.

When you can make your employees feel recognized and important, you'll succeed.

PERSONAL PROBLEMS

Don't be surprised if you're asked for advice by your employees regarding personal problems. Believe it or not, because you're a manager, you're expected to know the answers to questions about legal, finances, roommates, babies, cars, and relationships, even if you are single and younger than your employees. I mean, you're the manager, so you know. Right?

It always seemed like a significant portion of my day was spent answering personal problem questions. Don't be surprised if you get 10 questions every day. This is very time consuming but do the best you can.

Caution: don't get drawn in and feel personally responsible. This will only drive you crazy. Keep in mind that it is their problem. You're just trying to help. Don't get deeply and personally involved. Again, just do the best you can.

AVOID. JUST SAY NO.

Believe it or not, you'll eventually be asked to co-sign for a car or truck.

One word: Don't.

Most restaurant managers are empathetic and want to help their employees. But, no matter how sad or desperate the employee's story sounds, do NOT co-sign for a car. Over the years, I have seen a couple of well-meaning managers shocked to find that soon after co-signing, the employee took the car and was never seen or heard from again. These managers were left paying for a car/truck every month for years. Imagine how you'd feel if you were taken advantage of like that. Fun times. Not.

MEETINGS

You might think that the best way to get information to your staff is by calling a mandatory meeting. But you'd be wrong.

The best way to get information out to your staff is by holding shift meetings before each shift and of course, one on ones while working a shift. Shift meetings are usually the better way to share information. They'll take a little more time to reach everyone, but they are easy, painless, and cost effective with better results than mandatory meetings. Mandatory meetings have all sorts of disadvantages. First, it is federal law that employees must be paid to attend mandatory meetings. This makes them very expensive and should be reserved for rare, extraordinary events. They are also a pain in the butt for everyone because it upsets their schedules causing massive resentment unless the meeting is seriously serious.

BEWARE THE LINE

There's an invisible line that a manager must balance with employees between being too friendly and too distant. This is always tough to navigate, but you'll usually know it when an employee crosses this line. When it happens (and it will happen), you've got to pull away and establish boundaries.

Like most managers, I had my favorites. They were easy to talk to and always did a great job; I only had to ask, not tell, and they would do whatever it was I asked of them. But over time, one of them would inevitably say something that struck me as just too familiar, making me uncomfortable. This can take many forms, from being too casual around you at work, to asking me to go for a drink, or assume that I would let them eat something that they knew they shouldn't. They crossed an invisible line where they assumed a friendship and familiarity beyond manager/employee. It is hard to put into words, but I would know when it happened, and I'm sure you will too. When it does happen, just back off. Be a little more distant, a little less available, and a bit more formal around them. They'll notice and it usually takes care of itself. If it doesn't, you'd best address them individually and be direct.

DIFFERENT MANAGER, DIFFERENT MORALE

One of my students was a part-time server for a national restaurant chain while he went to college. He loved working there because a restaurant has just about everything that a young man needs. Excitement, flexible schedule, friends, and a great way to make money. He was able to buy a Jeep and life was pretty good.

What concerned me was when he talked about the way the general manager managed the restaurant. Unfortunately, this general manager was not isolated, and he was not the exception. In fact, he represented the old school type of managing that only reinforced the worst that restaurants have to offer. Abusive, callous management has no place today (or yesterday). Is there any wonder why turnover can be high?

He mentioned that once the GM came into the service area and yelled: "Attention! Attention! I have something to say. William, over there, is going to pay for the food that he is playing with on the counter." When William protested that it was not his food, that it was dead food that had been laying there for over an hour and that he was just stirring it, the GM said again that he was going to pay for it as an employee meal. All the staff heard this and couldn't believe how unfair he had been. As a direct result, two servers applied to a competing restaurant and all the employees who heard this outburst reacted by having less respect for the GM.

Of course, this wasn't the first time for this GM. One day the server had a party of 13 in his station. The GM came over to him and said that he was going to seat a party of 15 in a minute. The server told him that he didn't think he could take another big party at this time. The GM started to object when he suddenly said, "forget it" and walked away. The server felt bad about this and after a few minutes told the GM that he would take the table, but it would be rough, and he would need some help. The GM said again to forget it, that he had someone else to take it, someone who was obviously stronger.

Is there any reason to make an employee feel guilty about being honest with their ability to handle two large parties? No, of course not. This employee told me that there was such a tremendous difference in employee morale depending upon who the manager was. Unfortunately, this is typical when managers only know one way to manage.

PRIZES

It might be tempting to have a contest and hand out prizes because you think it will help morale. But be careful! You've got to think through prizes. Can everyone win or have you made it so that only a few can really win? Are all your contests focused on servers leaving out everyone else? Prizes can be great to encourage behavior, but they can also do the opposite by alienating many if you're not careful.

Prizes should be for one reason and one reason only and that is to drive behavior a certain way. The usual reasons are to help encourage raising the check average or to encourage dessert or wine sales.

A small note on prizes itself. Not everyone wants what you want. You might think that 2 tickets to Lady Gaga would be great, but others might want to lose that particular contest. You want everyone to be able to win and you want them to want the prize. Otherwise, you're just wasting money from your budget because employees who don't care, don't participate.

Consider having a choice of 3 prizes – cash, concert tickets, and movie tickets, for example. Or consider adding a prize that would be actually useful, like bus fare for a month, free ESL classes, a gas card, or a class at the local community college along with the concert tickets, etc. You just never know what will trigger enthusiasm. You might want to offer a fun prize, practical prize, and one other.

JOB HATE

Do you know how many of your employees hate their jobs? When employees hate their jobs, they significantly affect everyone around them. Employees who hate their jobs are most likely to develop the following behaviors:

- They are apt to quit at any moment. Many become very sensitive, with the slightest annoyance causing them to quit on the spot. Having an employee walk off in the middle of a shift can ruin your day.

• They can steal. They justify theft by feeling they are owed or simply to get back at management.

• They are more apt to be rude to customers, acting out their feelings of anger and frustration.

• They'll resist anything that they don't want to do.

• But the worst is that their attitudes rub off on good employees. This eventually makes even good employees bad. This is a phenomenon that I have always found amazing. How can one employee with a bad attitude negatively affect so many good employees? You'd think it would be the other way around, but unfortunately, that is usually not the case.

When bad employees are not dealt with, when management tolerates bad behavior, every employee notices. Management sends a clear message that they have no standards.

SO, WHAT TO DO?

Talk to them in private about how you perceive their attitude and about how they are coming across. If they truly have a bad attitude, you can have "the talk". Simply say that the choice is theirs. Either get with the program or they won't be there long.

COMMAND AND CONTROL

Are you the type of manager that must use the management style of command and control?

You know who you are.

You go through the restaurant and grill servers on the menu, how many ounces is this, give me the description of our house red, describe one of the seafood dishes. Of course, you don't ask them in a developmental way. You interrogate them. You do this because you believe it shows that you are serious about training and service. You believe you are doing it because it will help sales and service through a more knowledgeable service staff. But does this approach really help? Typically, it does in the short term, but does not in the long term and does more lasting damage.

Intentions are good, but the old command and control style of management belongs in management theory classes or, better yet, management history classes.

What's the alternative? Coaching. The difference between coaching and the traditional restaurant management style of command and control is tremendous. Command and control is telling and telling is one-way communications.

I teach, you listen.
Because I know and you don't know

Coaching is two-way communications with questioning, observations, and feedback at its center. The old way blocks any kind of meaningful communications with your employee while coaching encourages two-way communications. Just as important, however, is the fact that coaching places both the coach and the employee on the same level. This makes for a sense of employee buy-in and ownership of the training rather than the employee learning a task or becoming defensive. Believe it or not, your employees love to be trained and developed. Plan your training in such a way that it is practical. Explain why you want them to learn the material. Explain it in a manner that shows respect, rather than talking down to them.

One of the most important reasons that employees, especially our 16 to 25-year old's, stay or leave is because of how they feel about management. If their managers talk down to them, berates them, or humiliates them at work, they'll be gone. They can and will leave to go to restaurants that respect employees. All you have to do is compare turnovers to see that this is true.

PROBLEM EMPLOYEES

You told them. You showed them. You trained them. You told them again. And, still, they do it wrong. What is going on? For managers, this is frustrating. This is when you might want to have "The Talk". Obviously, it would be easy to write them up each time they screwed up. Then, after a certain number, usually 3, it would be adios. But try this before it gets to the adios.

There is usually some reason or reasons that employees screw up. So, sit them down and ask them. Point blank. "Why do you keep doing _____? What's going on?" Often, you'll find that there *is* something going on that has nothing to do with management or the restaurant. Quite often, just by listening and taking a personal interest, you might turn around an employee from one of the worst to one of the best. It happens. Try it.

THE HAWTHORNE EXPERIMENT

Almost a hundred years ago (1924-1927) experiments were carried out on a group of workers at the Hawthorne Electric plant in Illinois. At first, management thought that increasing lighting would increase productivity. As they increased lighting, productivity did go up. But as the lighting went down, the workers productivity increased until they were working almost entirely in the dark with productivity still going up. What they found was that lighting had nothing to do with productivity, but it did have everything to do with the attention that was given the workers. Employees today are no different. Caring, feedback and attention are still vitally important.

TRAINING

The restaurant industry tries to ensure the quality of service by providing the best training that it can. But sometimes this doesn't work because our training tends to treat each customer the same. Too bad people are not the same.

GOLDEN RULE VS PLATINUM RULE

Since all customers don't want to be treated the same, why not treat customers differently? You probably know the golden rule, but do you know the platinum rule? The golden rule is to treat others like you want to be treated. The platinum rule is to treat others the way they want to be treated. A much better rule since one size does not fit all.

One table wants their server to be talkative, friendly, and casual while the other table doesn't want a new best friend, they just want a more formal service with minimal contact.

Good service is what the customer wants. Training should incorporate this to recognize what the customer wants and the flexibility to give the kind of service that they want. Your customers will thank you.

KA KA

Early in my career, I tried to treat all my employees the same, whether they were the best or worst, good or bad. After a while, I noticed that the bad employees realized there was no penalty for being a slacker and took advantage of me. But what was worst was that the good employees realized they were being taken advantage of by following the rules.

They were right and I couldn't blame them. I mean, do the right thing, or do the wrong thing and still get treated the same? What a deal! It took me a while to realize that doesn't make sense because I could tell that even the good employees weren't as good as before. I was actually making good employees worse and the bad employees even worse. It took some time, but I finally wised up. So, Ka Ka method was born.

This simply identifies who the best, average, and worst employees are. Draw a bell curve with the worst employees on one end with KA, the OK employees in the fat middle, and the best employees at the other end with another KA.

The KA with the worst means you should **Kick Ass** the worst employees, but for the best employees, you want to **Kiss Ass**. Basically, do what you can for the best employees, such as rewarding them with priority scheduling. Just going through the process of identifying your best and worst employees will be eye opening.

KA KA is just a tool to recognize (and remind) that some employees perform better than others. Some are great employees while some are average or below average. Caution: Make sure your employees know what factors you think makes for a great employee and what does not.

TOLERATING BAD BEHAVIOR AND ATTITUDE

Customers tend to blame the individual server or host rather than the real cause, which is invariably, management.

I remember holding a customer service workshop made up of restaurant managers and asking them to describe their employees. It was very interesting to hear them passionately describe their own employees as lazy, uncaring, low standards, no work ethic, and an only in-it-for-themselves attitude.

I wrote each trait on a blackboard on either the 'good' side or the 'bad' side. Not surprisingly, the 'bad' side was full, while the 'good' side was almost empty. That finished, I turned around and told them that the reason that their employees were like that was simple. The problem didn't lie with the employees, but rather with themselves, the managers.

The managers either tolerated bad employees or they made their employees that way and then tolerated them. Either way, they had the power to identify problem employees and either train, develop, or fire them, but they obviously chose not to.

> No one applying for a job starts with a bad attitude, tries to be late, wants to cause problems, and not care.
>
> New employees **want** to do a good job; they **want** to have a good attitude. It is management's job to keep them that way

Research has shown that it is management that is the number one cause of employee turnover. Every manager has the capability to have excellence in his or her restaurant. Want to get noticed? Want to establish pride? Take charge of your restaurant and establish excellence.

PART TIMERS

How do you view your part-time employees? Do you see them as temporary employees who will quit at the drop of a hat, have no vested interest in their job, and who don't see the "big picture"? If that is the case, then part time morale is going to be an issue and anytime morale is an issue, customer service cannot be at its best.

Every restaurant has its share of full-time and part-time employees. Many restaurant managers give preference to full-time employees giving them better shifts, better stations and more understanding and tolerance when problems occur. With their part-timers, some managers can be very policy oriented, black, and white with rules, and intolerant with part-timers when problems occur.

That is too bad, because they are not only alienating the part-time employees with different standards but setting up an attitude in their employees that can only act itself out negatively usually as a self-fulfilling prophesy of bad morale, low expectations and high turnover.

The fact is that part-time employees can be your best employees. After all, they don't usually burn out and they should have the best attitudes since they view the customers as their ticket to achieving their money goals.

Some guidelines in dealing with your part-timers:

1. Keep them part time.

Honor their schedule requests. Don't schedule them for more than they said they can work. Even in your worst bind, resist pressuring to over-schedule them. But, when you do get in a bind, just ask. Don't threaten and don't demand. Many will be glad to add shifts to help you out. Just don't expect it each week; make it the exception. They want to be part timers, so let them be part time. Make sure that when interviewing, you are very specific about the future schedules: "Here's the schedule you will most likely have". Don't set up false expectations that are not realistic. This is probably the number one reason that causes more terminations and ill will than all the others combined. If in school, they have a social life, classes, homework, and tests to balance with work. If not in school, kids, husbands, wives, or parents require their time and attention. Many times, it is a delicate balance that adding a shift will be too much, forcing them to leave and look elsewhere.

2. Have the same expectations and standards for part-timers as you do with full-time employees.

It is essential to be fair and consistent with all rules for everyone. Part-timers will overlook a lot of flaws if they know that everyone is treated the same.

3. They want to feel that they are part of the team.

Communicate with them. Spend the time to get to know them as individuals and not just a body that you need to staff the restaurant.

4. Keep your restaurant fun.

Professionalism and fun can coexist. Just like the basics of food service, with hot food served hot, big things should be treated as big, but small things should be treated as small.

Part-timers can be one of your most valuable assets. They are usually motivated, eager to come to work, and want to be part of the team. Just treat them with respect and as individuals. But most importantly, treat them equally.

REVENGE IS NEVER GOOD

In all my years in management, I only had one employee who ever walked out in the middle of a shift. Only one, and, of course, that was one too many. I had just been transferred to this restaurant and it happened in the middle of a rush. It took a few minutes to realize he was gone. And then a couple more minutes to realize the guy was really gone. I was so mad. He had hurt me, the restaurant, customers, and his fellow servers since to get it sorted out, extra tables had to be given to the stronger servers. Anyway, I was really mad.

When this happened, I was in Texas. Texas had a rule that if an employee quit or was fired, the employee must receive their final check within 72 hours. This guy came in to collect his check and I told him it would be in tomorrow. When he came in the next day, I told him his check would be in the next day. After a few days of this, I got a call from the friendly Federal Wage and

Hour Board. They told me in very definite terms that this employee better have a check in the next 24 hours or the restaurant would be fined. I tried to explain that the guy had walked out in the middle of a busy shift. I was told that the employee better have his check within 24 hours. The moral of this story is that you should not take it personally. Just do your job and do what the law says to save yourself stress and negative emotions. It is just not worth the few minutes of revenge.

FIRING EMPLOYEES

In 16 years in restaurant management, I think I only fired 2 or 3 employees because all the others quit. I know, that sounds like BS. But I am a believer that when employees are screwing up so much that you think about firing them, there must be something else going on with them.

When an employee under performs, sit them down in private and first ask if they enjoy what they are doing. When you think about it, isn't it impossible to be good at anything that you hate? If (or when) they admit they are miserable in their job, try to find out why. It might have nothing to do with you, other management, or the company at all. It could be financial, personal, or family problems, all far from work problems.

If they open up to you about what is really happening to them, you might be able to turn them around simply by listening and trying to understand where they are coming from. However, if they just hate the job or management, you should remind them that they will hate coming to work even more next week and even more the week after that. Why stay miserable? Encourage them that it might be best to move on to another job or even another industry. People who don't like what they do are destined to fail. In the long run, you'll be doing them and your company a favor. Life is too short to work where you hate.

TURNOVER

The hospitality industry has a justifiably horrible reputation for having high turnover compared to other industries. Most managers don't know much about turnover, much less know what their own turnover is.

Many managers believe that high turnover is just a part of the restaurant industry. They accept high turnover as inevitable, just like they accept death and taxes. They believe that if an employee leaves, there's always someone else to take their place. I don't accept any of that, never have, and never will because management can reduce turnover.

What is Turnover?

Turnover refers to the number of employees who leave your restaurant, whether by getting fired or by resigning. The basic problem with turnover is that you've got to replace an employee who leaves. This means management must recruit applicants, interview them, and then train them. Each of these steps cost time and money, plus each step is an extra hassle for management.

You're never going to get to zero turnover and not all turnover is bad. Not all turnover is bad because some employees should leave if they are bad employees and because employees leave for very legitimate reasons, such as having to quit to take care of someone, taking a better job, or graduating and moving away. You're just trying to get it as low as possible.

Here's a closer look at high turnover:

Expensive

The good news is that your departmental labor budget probably has some turnover built into it in the form of training dollars. (Ask your GM how much). But what is not inevitable is high turnover, which causes your labor to go over budget. It costs money to recruit and train employees. This gets expensive because not only do you have to spend money on the trainee, but you also must pay the trainer of the trainee. Together, this can kill your labor budget.

Stress

High turnover always means added stress on managers. When turnover gets out of hand, the restaurant is shorthanded, sometimes drastically shorthanded. Managers will have to help bus, bartend, cook, and wait tables, in addition to managing. As you can imagine, this is very stressful for managers knowing that their shift will totally suck. In the middle of all this, managers also have to take time out to interview applicants and monitor those that they hire. Your employees hate it because they know they'll be asked (and sometimes forced) to work extra shifts, take additional tables, or work longer hours. At first, they won't mind because of the extra money, but if it continues, they'll resent the extra hours causing some to quit, making it even worse.

Lowers morale

If you have a high turnover rate, there is likely low employee morale. Each shift is tough, lasts forever, and are always shifts from hell. If being shorthanded is a short-term thing, employees will usually be great and pitch in to help in any way they can. But when it goes on and on, morale goes straight down, and you'll see even higher turnover.

How to figure turnover

To do anything about turnover, you've first got to know what your turnover is.

All you need are 3 numbers. The number of employees at the beginning date (usually the beginning of a month), the number of employees at the end date (usually the end of the month), and the number of employees who left during that period of time.

Add the beginning and the end numbers together and then divide by 2 to get the average number of employees in the month. Now, just divide the number of employees who left by the average number of employees. Finally, multiply by 100 to get the turnover percentage. Here's an example.

March 1st - 20 employees

March 30th - 24 employees

Total 44/2 = 22 average

5 employees were terminated for various reasons during March

5/22 = 0.227

0.227 x 100 = 22.7% turnover

This can be done monthly, quarterly, or yearly.

The turnover percentage by itself really doesn't mean much without comparing it to something. In 2019, the US Bureau of Labor Statistics estimated the average turnover rate at 78.6% for Accommodations and Food Service. As a comparison, Retail was 58%, Financial and Insurance was 24.9% and Education and Health was 29.3.

How does your department compare with the other departments or how does your restaurant compare to others?

THE POWER OF MANAGEMENT

Teaching hotel and restaurant students working in restaurants and hotels allows me to keep in contact with restaurant employees and, after they graduate, restaurant managers. I hear more often than I would like that many employees are unhappy, dissatisfied, and frustrated. They feel this way because managers have mistreated them.

I don't think we fully realize the power that bad management has on our employees. Bad managers can bruise each person they come into contact with which eventually numbs the wonder and joy that each person begins their job with. It makes for employees who think they are no more than 'disposable' employees. Typical examples:

- working too many hours
- close-open shifts
- not getting expected/promised bonuses or raises
- vacations earned but not granted or granted grudgingly
- paychecks that are a little off yet no priority to fix them
- performance evaluations not done on time
- quickly criticized and rarely praised

When good management does arrive on the scene, it takes an incredible amount of time, effort, and skill to undo the damage in trust, loyalty, and the individual's self-worth.

It is all such a waste. Literally hundreds of thousands of employees and an untold number of managers merely go about their jobs, pulling shifts, when they would like to do so much more-- not just *do* their job, but be enthusiastic and proud of it.

WHAT WOULD YOU DO?

You are a manager trainee, doing your position training with employees. While in training, you do the same work as they do and wear the same wear the same uniform. You've been in training for 3 weeks and this week you're in cook training. By the 4th day, you've come to know the cooks. They like you. You like them. You're on break with the cooks when they start bad-mouthing the general manager. One says, "The GM promised me a raise 4 weeks ago and I still haven't gotten it. I'm pretty mad about it".

The cook turns to you and asks, "What do you think about that? Don't you think that really sucks?"

How would you answer?

WHAT I DID

I asked the employee if he had gone to see the GM to tell him directly. This employee said that he had not because he figured the GM would just get mad. I told him that I doubted that but to find a slow time and talk with him.

REFLECTION

When you're doing your position training, you're doing the work of employees, you're in the same uniform, and with employees, but don't forget that you're still a manager.

When employees complain about another manager, you've got a few ways to answer them, but like a forward pass in football, there are 3 things that can happen, and two of them are bad.

The first answer that you could say is that you've just started and really don't know enough.

This seems safe, but don't do this. The employees really want to know what you think. If you avoid the question it makes you look weak and you'll start to lose credibility.

The second answer is the opposite of the first. You may want to fix the problem, so you say that you'll go to the GM and find out what is going on.

Don't do this! You have not built up any credibility yet. As a brand-new manager trainee, you don't want to tell a GM (who you don't know well) that you heard that the GM doesn't keep promises and is unfair. The GM will take what you say personally. Congratulations. You are now on the GM's shit list. And what if the GM asks you for the name of the employee who said this to you? Not a good position to be in. Totally lose-lose.

Probably the best way to handle this situation is to ask the employee if he has gone to the GM directly. If they haven't, tell the employee that the best way to resolve this is to go to the GM and tell the GM exactly what they told you. The employee will find out immediately what is going on. Often it is just that the GM has forgotten about it, apologizes, and fixes it. Either way, they'll know.

You haven't avoided the question and you've given good advice.

CHAPTER 5

CUSTOMERS: CAN BE PEOPLE TOO

Unfortunately, the typical day-in-the-life of a restaurant manager includes customer complaints. Many managers hate talking to customers anyway, but they *really* hate talking to ones with problems. Unfortunately, this is not only a part of a manager's job description, but also a fact of life.

The good news is that it can also be very satisfying to change a customer from hostile to loyal customer. This is a learned skill and should be looked at as a challenge to the manager's ingenuity, hospitality, and graciousness. Once you have this attitude, you'll love customer interaction, rather than hate it. Give this a chance. If you take finding out the problem and solving the problem as a personal challenge, you'll find this very satisfying.

START THE GUEST EXPERIENCE GOING THE RIGHT WAY

One of the major elements that form customers' experiences are their expectations when they go out to eat. Research has long proven that when a person has a positive expectation, their tolerance level is much higher than one who has a negative expectation.

As an example, a clean parking lot, followed by a clean lobby, followed by a helpful host will give the restaurant some slack if the appetizers come out a little slow. But if the opposite had been true with a dirty parking lot, followed by a dirty lobby, followed by a rude hostess, the appetizers would be doomed if they were even a minute late.

HANDLING CUSTOMER COMPLAINTS

Some suggestions to better handle customer complaints:

1. Get involved

Take a deep breath and go to them. Be relaxed, state who you are, ask for their name, then ask them what happened.

Emphasize to all servers, bussers, and hosts to let you know when they perceive that a customer is not pleased. This may sound like a terrible idea, especially for anyone who doesn't really enjoy engaging with customers. But often you can prevent a big problem from happening by catching it when it is a small problem. Customers are usually surprised and delighted to find an attentive and concerned manager.

Sometimes the problems are obvious, but often even when the customer says everything is "OK", the server or host may get the perception that the customer is not really satisfied. Encourage your employees to let you know immediately so that you can stop by their table. This goes for the hosts at the door too since that is your last chance to change a negative opinion. Your servers will appreciate your willingness to visit tables since their tips will probably go up. Every employee knows which managers find it a good time to inspect the walk-in when they sense a customer problem. You will get better and better at understanding customers and your confidence will grow as you handle them.

By visiting the customer you'll find out that either there wasn't anything wrong and you've gotten to know them, or you have prevented a small problem from becoming a big problem, and you've gotten to know them. Either way, your customers and your employees are happy.

> **IMPORTANT:** BEFORE you go to the table, delegate phone calls and other interruptions to someone else so that your entire attention can be devoted to the customer. If you want a rise in the level of anger and frustration for the customer, all you have to do is interrupt them with "excuse me," "Just a minute", or "What were you saying?" You have just entered "lose-lose" territory. Always listen without interruption or comments.

2. KNOW YOU can solve whatever is wrong

You do have the power and the authority to do that. This should give you confidence and be very empowering.

3. Have a positive attitude

Don't appear at the table, cross your arms, and say, "What's the problem here?" I've heard this myself when I have asked a server to get the manager when all I wanted to do was compliment the server. It really soured my positive attitude. It just begs the customer to unload on you.

4. Let the customer talk

Let them air out the whole situation. It allows the customer to tell their story with all the details and emotion that they feel is necessary. This step is vital to let the customer drain some of their emotion and anger. Don't say anything, except to give body language that you are listening intently.

5. Be empathetic

Express understanding with how they feel or were treated.

You're not admitting fault. You don't even have to agree with them, but you do have to communicate that you understand. Your tone of voice and body language go a long way to reinforce what you say. In fact, without the proper tone or body language, your words will sound hollow. I hate when a manager comes over to my table with their hands on their hips, challenging, " Is there a problem here?" when all I wanted to do was say hello and comment on the great time I was having. Emphasis on was.

6. Understand THE COMPLAINT

This is the main communication step. This is where you ask any questions that you need to get the complete picture of the negative experience. Ask relevant questions to clarify your understanding of the facts. Resist jumping to conclusions until you are satisfied that you understand the entire situation.

7. Believe the customer

Remember, they are telling you from their perspective. Sure, some customers will try to get over on you, but don't let that influence you. The vast majority are coming to you with a valid complaint. Most customers, believe it or not, are reasonable. They don't want to have a scene any more than you do. They don't want to appear petty or unreasonable. But when they feel they have been taken advantage of or ignored they will flame. If you assume the customer is truthful, you have just taken away a major source of stress related to service careers. The employee is not having a confrontation, nor are they conducting an interrogation; They are not looking for negatives but listening to what is being told to them without having to be a judge that must rule in favor of the company.

8. Don't take complaints Personally

Dealing with customer complaints can be draining. I've had several shifts totally ruined when I took complaints personally.

One danger of taking complaints personally is that it can affect your attitude for the rest of the shift bringing everyone down and making for a long shift. Even worse, this negative attitude can be brought home affecting your relationship there. Let it go.

9. Solve the problem quickly, quietly, and courteously.

Come to closure that you both feel good about. Remember the customer was telling you the truth. Tell the customer what you will do to rectify the situation. Make the customer feel good about the solution. Do not sound angry yourself or make the customer feel guilty. Even if you must break or bend policy, do what is right in the circumstances. Put yourself in their place. How would you have felt? How would you have felt if they were your parents?

Give them your business card and tell them the next time they come in to please ask for you. You'd like to make sure that they will be personally taken care of. They may or may not actually ask for you, but this reinforces that you have taken them seriously.

10. Follow-up

If possible, follow-up with the customer. Whether by e-mail, letter, or text, this step is impressive.

11. Take steps to fix the problem(s) that caused the problem in the first place

A good idea to keep a log or journal of customer complaints to enable you to see any trends. Your goal as an effective manager is to prevent problems.

CONFRONTATIONS

No one likes confrontations, including restaurant managers. It is easy to be intimidated by complaining customers. Some managers have only one tool and that is to comp. They just go through the motions by comping entire meals to appease the customer and end confrontations. They were going to do this regardless of the problem. At the end, the customer still may not be satisfied, but the manager just didn't want to deal with it anymore.

This is unfortunate. It is always so much easier to just do enough to get disgruntled customers out of sight. But to really turn around a bad situation, we really must push ourselves into listening to our customers and hearing what they say. Believe it or not, this is the absolute best time for a disgruntled customer to be converted into a loyal customer.

Don't treat a customer complaint as a confrontation. Most customers don't want confrontations either. Many customers just want to be listened to. When a manager sees them and listens, often that's all that's required. They just wanted to vent, now they are satisfied. No comps needed.

The next time you're in a restaurant, see if you notice a manager. In most situations, you probably won't. In fact, I hardly ever do. So, when I notice a manager's presence or a manager stops by, I'm impressed! You may not realize this, but for a customer, getting to know the manager is usually a big deal.

Keep in mind that the object is to really solve any problem that the customer has. Solving means that both parties are satisfied with the solution. It doesn't mean that you as a manager just stuck to company policy, but to make sure your customers leave satisfied, that management was concerned and solved their problem. This ex-disgruntled customer now knows one of the managers and believes you will take care of them in the future.

Don't take the easy way out by not talking with the customers, because it only makes for escalating the problem.

Push yourself, talk to your worst customers. Once you do it a couple of times, you'll learn that you can be very effective in turning lemons into lemonade. It is a great feeling to know you've made a loyal customer out of someone who potentially would have been lost. Using the direct approach is one aspect of management that will serve you well in your management career.

YOU ARE THE MESSAGE

What is your attitude when one of your employees come to you with a customer complaint? Do you look at the customers as complainers even if the cause of the complaint is dirty silverware or food cooked improperly?

Some servers have a low tolerance for customers who complain, even slightly. They feel that any complaint immediately qualifies the customer as a customer from hell.

After your interaction with the customer, be careful how you come across to the server, host, or bartender who had the complaint. If you roll your eyes after talking with a customer, your message is that the customer was wrong to complain, that complaints are petty and meaningless, and that management is only going through the motions. The server will pick up on your attitude and service will decline.

Your attitude is mirrored in your employees.

CUSTOMER VIEWPOINT

Put yourself in the customer's shoes. First, keep in mind that your customers made a choice to come into your restaurant, not your competition. They chose you. Second, trust them. Believe them.

Second, most people don't complain just to complain. They are not just pointing out a problem, they think they are doing something to help the restaurant to excel. Third, they have paid real money for the restaurant to meet the expectations that your restaurant has set. If you are not meeting your own expectations, don't you want to know so you can correct them?

Set the tone by wanting your servers to get you when they have a complaint. They will deeply appreciate this!

The right attitude

It is important that you make sure that your servers and hosts have the right attitude towards customers and especially customers who have a complaint. Emphasize to listen, respond, and learn from customer complaints. Take complaints seriously and encourage them to always tell you whenever there is even a potential complaint. Maybe most importantly is that you consider complaints helping the restaurant rather than a pain that you have to deal with.

Sure, customers from hell exist. We've all suffered the pain of enduring customers who had incredibly picky, petty, and even non-existent problems that we worked hard to solve, all the while knowing that they were unsolvable. But they are the exceptions. Most customers expect a good experience and even ignore most smallish problems or inconsistencies that happen during a dining experience.

When you buy shoes, or a toaster, or a book and it has a defect, you return it. You expect either a replacement or your money back. A restaurant is no different. Treat customers who have a complaint sincerely and with a sense of urgency. They know your restaurant can do better. They are trying to tell you something useful. Believe it or not, you need customers who are willing to tell you about problems. Just think about the alternative: customers who leave never tell you why they leave, the problem stays, and more customers will have the same problems. Why do this?

In my experience, most of the complaining customers turned out to be the nicest people. They just wanted to let the restaurant know and didn't expect anything in return at all. These are people who enjoy the restaurant who you never knew existed but have now made a connection and enjoy seeing week after week.

When you view complaining customers as people who want to help, you'll be surprised at how good the experience turns out when you visit them.

DRIVE BY, TOUCHING TABLES, AND "IS EVERYTHING OK"?

I sometimes see a manager passing by tables and asking, "Is everything ok?" Most customers answer, "yes, everything is ok". The manager is satisfied, smiles, and moves on to the next table.

Personally, I just want to scream. Major pet peeve of mine.

Is everything OK? Are you kidding? OK is the standard for your restaurant? OK means average, good enough, mediocre, not great, but not bad.

This implies that OK is the standard of service that you want. OK is good enough. If you don't want average service, maybe you shouldn't ask if everything is OK.

A BETTER WAY

Rather than asking a general question at a table, a far better way is to ask specific questions about what you see on the table. If you notice a particular dish, ask about it. If it happens to be one of your favorites, tell them, they'll love it. If something has not been completely eaten, ask about it.

Don't worry that you're just asking for complaints. You're not. The vast majority of customers will be pleased that you noticed and that you took the time to ask about their experience.

Chances are, you will get straight answers that are useful. It is usually a waste of time to try to "touch" as many tables as possible. This usually comes off badly as the manager races by doing her best to hit all the tables. This does not show management concern because there is no dialogue and no sincerity. It is far better to "touch" fewer tables, engage with a few meaningful questions, and get real answers. That shows management really does care.

> *Customers are always surprised when shown excellent customer service because they are simply not used to it.*

SEEING OPPORTUNITIES, NOT ANNOYANCES

Most managers love to eat out. Many of us like to tell the manager when we have had great service from their employees. But it never ceases to amaze me that the majority of times that I've asked my server to get a manager to come by when he or she has a moment, the manager comes out with an attitude. He'll come to the table, cross his arms, and ask very seriously, "What seems to be the problem?"

What kind of message does that question, and body language send to customers? It can only make a bad situation worse or cause damage to an otherwise positive situation. As in my case, all I wanted to do was compliment one of the employees. Nothing ruins a great opportunity to pass along a compliment to your employees than a defensive attitude by the manager.

BE CAREFUL OF THE MESSAGE YOU'RE SENDING

I was in a restaurant recently and complimented the manager about one of the employees while the employee was standing next to him. Instead of using this as a great opportunity to say thank you and praise the employee, the manager just looked at me and said "So, you must be a relative." The young hostess went from glowing to hurt and embarrassed. The manager had blown an opportunity to instill pride and actually turned a slam-dunk positive situation into a negative one. That employee's attitude was bruised by an insensitive manager and you can bet that she won't forget it. It won't take much more to cause her to quit and you can bet that she tells that story to all her peers.

Similar negative attitudes affect the customer. When a customer wants to see you regarding a problem, treat it as an opportunity, not a nuisance. **Remember that most customers wouldn't tell you if they didn't care.** Telling the manager can be a process that they know will take time. I'd bet that many loyal, regular customers started out as disgruntled customers who received exceptional personal care by a manager and employees.

The first rule of customer service is to believe your customer. Even on the rare occasions when you just know they're trying to pull something over on you, don't let this influence your attitude. Believe them. Most customers are telling you how they really feel. And isn't that the only thing that counts?

Here are some common negative behaviors that managers should **NOT** do:

• Say "yes but". This sends a clear message to your customer that you are not listening and being defensive.

• Look bored. Pay attention, LISTEN. Don't think about the phone call that is waiting or the change you need to make. If your customer feels that what he is saying is not important, whatever you say, or offer will not be enough. Sincerity and attention are needed.

• Don't handle it yourself, don't send a server or hostess. Even in the most empowered workplace, there is nothing more effective than a few words from the manager.

• Give excuses. Customers just don't care about your problems. Just apologize and make amends.

- Don't do anything. There are a few things in life that are better if ignored, but a customer complaint isn't one of them.

- Delay. It is easy to get busy and forget about the complaint or put it as low priority. Handle customer complaints immediately. Research has proven that when a complaint is resolved quickly, it will cost less, and the customer is more likely to be satisfied with the outcome.

ON A COMPLETELY DIFFERENT NOTE. WHEN A CUSTOMER FALLS OR GETS HURT

Most of the time when a customer falls, they'll say they're fine, no problem. Regardless of what they say, document everything. Where it happened, the time, what you know, names of employees who saw the incident, and what they said to you and what you said to them. Make sure you are very attentive, helpful, and sincere. Make sure you write in the manager notes, so that your GM hears about any incidents from you first, even if the incident seemed small at the time. Check with your GM how best to write this up.

Most of the time the incident ends there. But sometimes stuff happens. Customers go home, feel some pain, and the next day go to the emergency room or their doctor.

If this happens, they or their insurance carrier, will contact the restaurant. They'll want all sorts of information. You'll be thankful that you made notes covering the incident.

I believe most cases that result in customers suing restaurants are because managers did not give the customer the attention that they expected. Contrary to what some people think, most customers don't want to sue their restaurant. But, when they feel that management did not care, they will want to punish the restaurant. If the manager at the time of the incident had offered sincere help, there would be no lawsuit.

Take customer falls or other injuries seriously. Spending a few dollars or treating someone kindly will eliminate almost all lawsuits. You don't have to admit that it was the restaurant's fault to help.

NEGATIVE CUSTOMER BLUES

Life in the customer service world is full of stress and difficult customers. Dealing with negative customers is a fact of restaurant life, but the good news is that this seemingly "lose-lose" situation can be turned around. If it's handled correctly, difficult customers can be turned into some of the most loyal, long term customers you'll ever have.

CUSTOMERS ARE NOT ALWAYS RIGHT

As an end note, customers are not always right. I drew my personal line in the sand if a customer treated any employee with no respect or cursed them. When this happened, I would very politely, but firmly, ask them to leave.

WHAT WOULD YOU DO?

One of your servers, who says she is speaking for all servers, tells you that tips have been stolen from tables. They all think that Robert, one of your busboys is the thief. She says that all the servers are really upset. (There are no security cameras).

What are you going to do about it?

What you're thinking about:

- Do you tell Robert that the servers think he's stealing tips?
- Do you fire Robert?
- Do you tell everyone?

WHAT I DID

1. Got each manager to announce at each shift meeting that there is a problem with tips being stolen so be extra careful.
2. Got the GM to start a new policy that no busser can bus any table until server lets a busser know that it is ok to bus. This puts the responsibility on the servers and off the bussers.
3. Told servers to let manager know the second you have a missing tip
4. I did not tell Robert. Most people accused of theft, especially when they are innocent, will quit immediately because of lack of trust. Robert did not deserve that.

REFLECTION

When this happened to me, it turned out that it was the server herself who was stealing tips (her roommate told me). This taught me that it is best to be cautious when someone accuses someone else. Don't react immediately just because someone says something is true. You don't want to accuse anyone without proof. It is best to first put in place systems and procedures to prevent whatever problem is happening.

CHAPTER 6

KNOW THE SCORE: YOUR CURRENT REALITY

Two guys are sitting in front of a television watching a game. Another guy wanders in who doesn't have a clue who is playing. Doesn't matter. What's the first thing out of the new guy's mouth? It is always "What's the score?"

Everyone wants to know the score. While many managers *think* they know how the GM feels about them, it is vital to *know*. When I first started, I didn't think about or worry about how I was doing because I thought it would just work out. I thought that because my regular performance reviews were OK, that would be enough. And besides, I thought I was doing a great job anyway. What's to worry about?

But what if your GM doesn't think you're doing such a great job, yet you think you are? In that case, you would keep doing what you've been doing and digging a deeper hole that you didn't even know you were digging. Obviously, it is far better to know as soon as possible that you are going in the wrong direction. It will be much easier for you to change direction when caught early and the GM's negative perception might not be permanent.

In some cases, you might think the GM likes you and thinks you are doing a good job because the GM occasionally asks about your car, family, or favorite sports team. But this might not be so. This same GM might just slam you during your formal performance review. Bottom line? Best to know, not guess, how your GM perceives you.

> *Your GM's perception of you is the key*
> *to your survival and your success*

The sooner you know how you are doing, the sooner you can either *stop* doing what you *should* be doing or *start* doing what you *should* be doing. The GM plays such a critical part in the success of every assistant manager that great pains must be taken to understand the expectations of the GM. You've got to continuously know if you are meeting those expectations by being aware of signals that the GM gives out regarding your performance.

Ideally, the GM monitors your progress, reviews your performance, and then makes suggestions in a regular and timely manner. Because of this frequent feedback, even if you do start to screw up, only minor corrections will be necessary to get back on track and since you have only been doing it a short time, it shouldn't cause any real damage to your credibility as a manager.

Unfortunately, sometimes assistant managers do not receive open, timely, and relevant feedback. With no feedback, the potential for assistant managers to feel a false confidence is strong. But this may not be the case: all may not be well. The wise assistant manager will seek out clues in any and every way possible.

OK. IT'S IMPORTANT. I GET IT. SO, HOW DO I KNOW HOW I'M DOING?

Let's start with how *not* to do it. Don't wait until your regular performance review. This is not a great idea since you must wait at least a month to find out that for a month you have been screwing up! No, you want and need much more immediate feedback.

For a new manager, here's what to do:

1. Know the GM's expectations of you regarding matters of financial, employees, and customers. If you are not absolutely clear on each expectation, ask for a meeting to make sure that you are clear. It is surprising how many assistant managers wrongfully assume they know what they're supposed to do, what budget numbers they should hit, and what the GM considers urgent. If you are not completely sure you know, you've got to ask.

Go over each area of your responsibility with the GM. Find out which areas are doing well and which areas the GM think are problems that need immediate attention. Make sure you get exact budget percentages to hit and you know the GM's standards for each area. You want to be on the same page regarding standards. You don't want to find yourself working toward what the GM will ultimately find only average and you're thinking it's great.

2. Ask for a copy of the manager performance review. If you're new to the company, ask to see the management performance evaluation worksheet to see up close and personal the qualities that you'll be rated on. Go over the review template and make sure you understand each area. If you're not clear about any of the areas, ask your GM.

3. Ask for feedback in real time. Encourage your GM to give you feedback anytime you screw up. In addition, go a step further, get the GM to explain to you why other actions that you could have taken would have been a better way. Make it clear to your GM that you want and value the GM's insight on your performance. You want the GM's views especially when you do something new, how you did on a particular task, or how you might improve on the next task. You don't need to schedule time or a formal meeting. Just pull your GM aside after a shift and request a reaction to the shift or any specific situation that you're not sure if you handled it correctly. The GM should not mind this at all. In fact, most GM's will welcome and approve that you are trying to learn from their experience.

> **WARNING**
>
> Don't ask for feedback just to suck up to the GM. Don't ask for feedback for situations when you know you've done a good job or your question has an obvious answer. Only ask for feedback when you have a situation where you really want to learn; otherwise, your GM will see you as a suck-up which kills the impression that you are serious about becoming a better manager.

4. Use specific questions

Don't ask, "Do you have any feedback for me?" That's not a good question because what if the answer is no? You've learned nothing.

Do ask: "What's one thing I could improve?" or "What do you think I could have done differently?"

Either question makes it clear that you want to get better. If your GM answers with vague answers, don't hesitate to ask for examples to help you understand.

Have brief meetings every 2 weeks with your GM to discuss how you did the previous 2 weeks. Lengthen this to once a month if the meetings are going well. This isn't a formal meeting, just a casual check in with your GM. Checking in weekly might be too soon to see any results and could be too much of a pain for the GM. Monthly meetings could be too long to let something go if you've done it wrong. Of course, if the GM wants it at longer or shorter intervals, so be it.

Make sure you make it clear that you want just a very short meeting and that you want real feedback, especially negative feedback. That way, if you're way off, then you've only been way off for two weeks and it will be relatively easy to stop what you're doing and start what you should be doing. This will go a long way in getting the GM to see you as committed to doing a superior job and serious about your career.

Receiving feedback can be stressful because well, you're being criticized. But trust me on this, you want to know sooner rather than later if the GM has criticisms. Just ignoring or avoiding criticism is career suicide. You want to know so that you can do something about it. The more often you get feedback, the easier it gets to hear feedback. Early criticisms will prevent you from doing what you should not be doing and avoiding negative perceptions from forming with the GM.

• Ask for feedback in real time. Don't wait till the next shift or next week.

• Ask specific questions to get helpful information and examples.

• Feedback can be brief, informal coaching moments during or after shifts, in the walk-in, or just about anywhere.

WHAT TO DO, WHAT TO DO.

Many assistant managers just go about their job, plugging away, assuming they are doing a good job. But what if the GM isn't communicating with you? And what if you have no idea what the GM really thinks of you?

I have seen too many assistant managers who just pull shifts not really thinking about how they are perceived. There's a big difference when the GM has confidence in you and when you are doing just an adequate job and not being considered for promotion.

Know how you are perceived by the GM
so you can do something about it
rather than not know and just pull shifts

MORE THINGS TO DO

Past performance reviews.

If you've had a performance report in the past, take it out and examine how you were rated in each category. If you've had more than one, do they mention the same negative traits? Have you improved on each of the criticisms? Are you sure your GM knows that you have improved on each of the criticisms? Make sure you have real evidence to back up your progress, not just your opinion.

Consider what the reviews say. Break down the reviews between traits mentioned and or rated into Excellent, Average and Below average categories. Even if the review is in narrative format, you can still do this exercise by sifting through the words to find the action nouns and adjectives that will help you get a complete picture of the review.

Be aware of signs

These can be subtle, or they can hit you over the head, but be aware of signals sent by the GM. This awareness will allow you to know as early as possible how the GM perceives you. Ideally, the GM will give relevant feedback in a timely and constructive manner before there is a problem, but realistically, this is sometimes not the case. For example, do you find that you aren't invited to meetings that you would normally attend?

Know how you're doing at regular checkpoints.
Not when it's too late to change the GM's perception.

PATTERN OF SUCCESS

You are striving for a pattern of success. You started as a manager trainee. You excelled. Then you got promoted to assistant manager in charge of one area. You excelled. Then you were in charge of another area. You excelled. Then you went to another area. You excelled. That is a pattern of success. Most of the time, you can tell how someone is going to do in the future by looking at how that person did in the past. Your job is to excel each step of the way. You are trying to establish yourself as someone who cares about their management performance. Each month, you should be getting better, pushing yourself to learn something new, take on more responsibility; all to prove that you should be considered for more responsibilities and eventual promotion.

THE BIG DAY: PREPARING FOR YOUR PERFORMANCE REVIEW

Review all information about you that is in writing. Past performance reviews, emails, any project reviews that you have done in the past to give you a sense of how the GM perceives your performance. Also, think back about any problems that happened, such as when you were late for a shift or had a sloppy close. Any one of them could have had a tremendous influence on the GM's perception of you. Often these moments may have seemed insignificant at the time but could have been very significant in shaping your GM's perception of you.

LIST EVERYTHING THAT YOU ARE RESPONSIBLE FOR:

1. Past performance reviews.

If you have any ratings that are average or below average, have you improved? If yes, great. Make sure you have examples ready to show how you have improved. If no, you'd better have some seriously great reasons why you have not.

2. Financial (P&L responsibilities).

List each P&L category that you are responsible for. For example, if you are in charge of the bar, the categories might be liquor, beer and wine costs, bar supplies expense, bartender labor expense, over time, and training expenses. Are you within budget on each one?

3. Know WHY your numbers are the way they are.

Whether you are in budget (great job!) or if you are high in some areas, do you know why? If you don't know, you've got to find the reasons why you are high.

4. Have a plan to correct.

Have a plan to correct any area that was over budget. (More about this in the Numbers chapter).

5. Employees

Is your area fully staffed? Are you proactive in staffing? Do you have an ongoing training plan? Do you discipline consistently and fairly? Are schedules out on time? Are they all well trained? Morale good? Is turnover high or low? Are your standards high and consistent? Do you play favorites? What is customer feedback?

6. Facilities

Is your area always clean, organized, labeled, and efficient?

7. Personal

Do you always act professional? Do you dress well? Are you always on time? Do you work well with your fellow assistant managers, staff, and employees? Do you bring your personal problems into work? Can your peers, employees, and general manager always count on you to do what you say you will do? Every time? Do you procrastinate?

8. Shifts

Are checklists followed and nothing ever missed? Do you communicate well with other management? Do your shifts go smoothly? Do you make sure the incoming manager is well set up?

9. Customers

Are you comfortable dealing with upset customers? Do you initiate talking with customers?

10. Intangibles

Do you try to anticipate problems, or do you find yourself going from crisis to crisis putting out fires? Do you try to see the "big picture", or do you just work the shift?

After doing the above, grade yourself objectively on each area. Keep your ratings simple with just 3 choices: Excellent, Average and Below average. Every item is not equal, but don't worry about weighting them, just rate as honestly as you can.

Then for each category that is average or below average, come up with a plan to get each above average.

DURING YOUR PERFORMANCE REVIEW

Listen. Do NOT be defensive. Do NOT be aggressive. This is a shared, candid experience. You're prepared, you've done the homework.

ASSESSING YOUR POWER

Regardless of your position, how much power do you have in your organization? Don't confuse power with authority. Authority is a formal right over people that comes with your title of the job. It is given to you by your organization and how much authority comes with the title. As you progress up the company ladder, your authority grows and goes right along with you.

Power, on the other hand, is given by your peers or subordinates, and is earned, never given. Power can be obtained from some skill, such as being the only person who knows how to program or by connections, like being the boss's nephew. Power cannot be given and it cannot be taken with you. If you get transferred or take a new job, you can't take power with you. You must start over again with zero power and re-earn it.

That said, do you think your sense of power grew in the last 6 months or a year? Do other assistant managers value what you say? Do they seek you out for advice? Does the GM talk to you about issues facing the restaurant? This is the real measure of how others perceive you. Has your power grown? If it hasn't, why hasn't it? If it hasn't, it might be one indication that something is wrong.

BEHAVIOR TOWARDS YOU BY THE GM

Has the GM's behavior over the past months been the same towards you? Have there been any "defining moments" in your relationship with the GM that make you concerned about how you are viewed?

Ideally, your GM coaches you continuously and cautions you the moment he sees you starting down the wrong path. Unfortunately, we don't always get the ideal GM. Some will just document every time you screw up.

It is best to know as early as possible when you perform below expectations and why. Unfortunately, many managers just wait until their regular performance review. Ignorance is not bliss because by then, it could be too late to change the GM's perception of you.

Knowing early is not always easy. Too often we are uncertain or unaware of what others think about us or we have such a high opinion of ourselves that we can't see anything negative. But the real question is: what does the GM think of your performance?

It is a great help to your career to know how you come across to others, but it is vital to know, and not guess, how you're perceived by your GM.

MICHAEL, ASSISTANT MANAGER

Michael was an assistant manager who worked hard every day. He arrived early, stayed late, lived and breathed his work. He felt he had great relationships with the GM, other managers, and the employees who he supervised. He had been on the job for about a year and was feeling confident that he was next to be promoted.

Michael was surprised when he was told that he had a meeting with his GM and the supervisor the next day. At the meeting, he received no praise for doing a good job; in fact, he was told that he had been doing a bad job. A long list of his shortcomings were given to him and he was consequently given the choice of termination or resigning.

Michael was devastated. How could he have been so blind? He was smart, quick, and, he thought, very aware of his performance. How could this have happened to him?

HINDSIGHT

There had been warning flags all around Michael from the time he started. As is typical, the warning signs started out as subtle but gradually became more frequent and more obvious, even to other managers and employees.

Michael loved technology and loved showing how much he knew. He would stop and help the admin assistant with software problems and help with any POS functions. He would spend enormous amounts of time revising systems or playing with the

POS. He thrived on the administrative and systems side of operations. His GM was heard to say many times that he got frustrated with Michael spending so much time making some systems overly complicated when they worked just fine.

Michael had been his own worst enemy by being overconfident. This made him oblivious to warning signals that became more and more apparent to almost everyone. Michael had been fixed in his own rosy picture of his job performance and was blind to even the most negative, glaring signals.

Stop and think what does your GM consider as priorities and what does the GM consider most important? In Michael's case, the GM was very operations oriented, liked to keep busy, and micromanage. The GM looked upon technology, systems, and paperwork as secondary, certainly not as a priority of the job.

Stay in close contact with your GM. This will keep your priorities consistent with your boss' priorities. Like Michael, we can get sidetracked or gravitate to parts of our job that we are most comfortable when it may be of only minor importance to your GM. Your actions and priorities must be in harmony with the boss's priorities.

> **WARNING:** When you misread your GM, it can only lead to problems. Michael strayed from what was important to his GM. Michael's computer and administrative skills did nothing for his credibility with the GM. They did nothing to enhance his power and reputation as he had assumed. It didn't make any difference that Michael was helpful and everyone else was impressed. Michael's GM was not impressed.

The GM was not impressed because of a fundamental difference in job expectations. Michael saw his computer activities as him doing **MORE** than expected but the GM saw the activities as causing him to do **LESS** on his main priorities.

WHAT WOULD YOU DO?

You've just gotten a great job with the best restaurant chain, gone through management training, and are now a new assistant manager. You arrive at your new restaurant excited, ready, and eager to do a great job

But, when you get there, you find that the General Manager ignores you and gives you the worst schedules. You are surprised and disappointed because you never thought that this could happen to you. You love your job and your employees, so you shake it off and get to work, still determined to do a great job.

After a few more months, you find that nothing has changed. When you make suggestions, the GM kind of listens, but nothing ever happens. At weekly manager meetings, you're basically ignored, never given any projects to do, never asked any questions. The other assistant managers seem to have good relationships with the GM, but you get nothing, no feedback, no praise, not even criticism.

You think you are doing a good job, but you are now getting depressed and sometimes angry. You thought this situation would get better, but after several months, you're not sure if you can take it anymore. You find yourself not caring. You know you're not doing a good job, but it doesn't seem to matter if you do a good job or bad job.

You've thought about quitting and looking for another job. You still like and believe in the company and would like to stay, but you're not sure what to do.

WHAT I DID

When this happened to me, I was so depressed that I almost decided to look for a new job without talking to the GM. But, once I had made this decision, I figured that I had nothing to lose, so I wanted to ask the GM directly, since he was the only person who could tell me.

Before I talked with him, I wanted to be prepared with all the information that I could about my past performance. I went through my P&L responsibilities; reviewed past manager's notes to see if there was anything that I had forgotten; I reviewed my staffing, shifts, and the overall quality of my areas and responsibilities, such as ordering, cleanliness, customer comments, and others.

Doing this verified that I had been doing a good job; I was now both angry and aggressive.

Since I had made my mind up that I was going to quit anyway, I had nothing to lose, so I went to the GM and requested a formal, off premise meeting. I said that I needed to know how I stood with him and the company. He was a little surprised but agreed to the meeting.

In the meeting I started off saying that I had the impression that I wasn't doing a good job and that I didn't have a future with the company.

I laid out all the information one by one. At the end, I said that I appeared to be doing a good job. Why didn't he?

REFLECTION

In my case, the GM was truly surprised. He could see how frustrated I was. He said that he thought I was doing a good job and promised to do a better job at communicating with me. This intervention, that I almost didn't have, saved a needless job change.

WHAT TO DO

- This could be painful, but the very first thing you should do is to objectively review yourself.
  - Go through your P&L responsibilities. Are you within budget in each area?
  - How is your department doing? Is it staffed? Good morale? Have your schedules been posted on time?

- Have your shifts run smoothly? Ordering done well, customers handled well, discipline and morale good?
- What have you done to make the restaurant better?
- Ask for advice from the other assistants

With this information, do your own performance review. What are your strengths and weaknesses? Then make a formal appointment with the GM. You've got to know what is going on and why. You need to have The Boss Talk (see chapter The Boss Talk).

CHAPTER 7

MANAGE UP

Your relationship with your GM is incredibly important. The GM has strong influence over your career since the GM sees you in action every day and communicates your performance to his boss who probably makes promotion decisions. If you want to receive good performance reviews and promotions, you've got to establish a good relationship with this most important person in your work life. You do this by "managing up".

MANAGING UP IS NOT SUCKING UP

Managing up is not sucking up or manipulating your GM. Don't give compliments to your GM if they are not deserved. Most GM's will see exactly what you are doing, and you will immediately lose credibility.

BUT FIRST, AN IMPORTANT POINT.

To be promoted, it is not enough to be the best assistant manager. This may seem strange but just being a great assistant manager will not always get you promoted. Will your best cook make a great kitchen manager? Maybe. But, then again, maybe not. The kitchen manager must grasp the entire kitchen, including costs, people management, and so much more. Sometimes the best cook either can't or doesn't want the added responsibilities or want the hassle of adding skills required to move to the next level. This is the same with assistant managers.

THEN WHAT DO I HAVE TO DO?

Your first goal is to get the GM to have the perception that you are someone who *can* be promoted. The next step is for the GM to perceive that you are *ready* to be promoted. Both are about the GM's perception of you. So, what do you have to do to get the GM to have that perception?

You must show the GM that

> *You are serious about your job.*
> *You want to get better.*
> *You want to do a great job.*

ARE YOU THINKING LIKE A GM?

If you're not already thinking like your GM, you should be. Getting into the mind of your GM is the only way to know what is expected of you by the only person who really matters in your professional life. Many people refuse to accept the basic fact that, like it or not, your GM controls your professional destiny. This is especially true when you are an assistant manager. But you can affect this destiny by ensuring that your boss perceives you as promotable. You can do this by *anticipating* and then *exceeding* his or her expectations.

Thinking like a GM requires you to think objectively. Start by imagining yourself in the position of the GM and handing out an assignment to one of your assistants. What would you think if you checked and the task assigned was sloppy or late?

You'd probably think that the assistant did not take the assignment seriously. Why wouldn't they have taken the trouble to do it right? Would you think this person was ready to be promoted? Of course not.

Would it matter if the assistant had stayed late to work on it? Or had never missed a day? Or had never been late?

No.

Managing up means first understanding your boss and then actually managing him or her. This may sound negative and a form of manipulation. It is not. Managing up leads to the best possible results for yourself, your GM, and your company.

Many very capable people who are normally very aggressive and capable in their jobs hurt their careers by being passive around their GM. They think they are giving the GM respect, but this actually hurts your image because the GM will think that the assistant manages in the same way. In other words, passive and weak, instead of aggressive and strong. The GM's perception of them will be as a weak manager. This is not a perception that gets you promoted. The bottom line is to act confident and be yourself around the GM.

The assistant who understands the GM has a marked competitive edge. Assistants who don't understand their GM have put on a blindfold that severely limits their effectiveness and makes it doubly difficult to be perceived as promotable.

In a perfect world, your boss is totally in touch with your needs and expectations and you with your GM's. However, in reality neither always occur. You have to be proactive to get to know what your GM's expectations of you are and know how to best use that information. Your career is truly a joint venture, but remember, that it is your GM's sense of reality that matters most, not yours.

This joint dependency creates dynamics that should be known and understood. They start with understanding that your boss is dependent on you just as you are dependent on him. GM's need your drive, honesty, and ability; otherwise, they can be severely hampered in their effectiveness. At the same time, you need the GM for support, information, and resources.

An even greater reason to manage up is for what the GM can do for your career in the longer term. Your GM is the direct link between you and the rest of the organization. Cut off this link and you have effectively cut yourself off from any chance of promotion.

Your GM's perception of you as promotable requires that you gain an understanding of your GM as well as understand your own present situation.

> *Understanding your GM is critical to your success. It is the only way to know what is expected of you by the only person who really matters in your professional life.*

The reality is that your GM controls your professional destiny. But you can affect this destiny by ensuring your GM perceives you as promotable.

IT IS CRITICAL THAT YOU UNDERSTAND YOUR GM'S JOB.

Many average assistants don't give their GM's problems a second thought, only concentrating on their own job. But promotable assistants attempt to understand the pressures of the GM's job. They seek to understand the GM's objectives and goals, helping to understand the GM's frustrations. Knowing the GM's frustrations and pressures allows for the proactive assistant to anticipate actions that could help the GM reach their goals and hopefully relieve some of the pressure.

You will be promoted because your GM believes that you can handle the next level, not because you stayed late or were exceptional at your job. We have all known great employees who were exceptional at their jobs, but when promoted, were terrible.

Don't be under the misconception that you have to be the best at your position. It is essential for you to develop the behaviors and skills necessary for your GM to view you as capable of taking the next step. Developing a reputation as a can-do, positive person who anticipates problems and acts to prevent them, completing projects ahead of schedule, ability and willingness to accept additional responsibilities are all valuable to your promotion and your GM's perception of you. Without the GM believing you can handle the responsibilities of the next level; you will never be promoted regardless of how technically proficient you are.

DON'T GET TOO COMFORTABLE

All of us have cycles in our jobs that cause our performance to go up and down. It is easy to get lulled into this up and down rhythm because events happen that cause us to lose our focus causing our performance to go down. Everyday pressures at home, often out of our control, such as illnesses, children, divorce, money problems, or home repairs can cause these lapses.

But more commonly, lapses are caused by getting into a routine, getting too comfortable, and going on autopilot. When performance falls even slightly it gets noticed. Unfortunately, this could be when opportunities for promotion are near. If you are at a low point or on a downward curve, you could be passed over. Even a slight dip may cause your GM to have doubts and shift you out of the running for promotion.

Promotable assistants maintain a consistently high level of job performance by not allowing the normal peaks and valleys to happen.

The difference between mediocre and excellent work is only about 10%. It's not much, but that 10% is typically the difference between promotable assistants and average assistants. If you can consistently condition yourself to do excellent work and not just "good enough" work, you are well on your way to becoming promotable.

Very simply, do all work to the best of your ability. Why? Because of the satisfaction that you will feel in the short term and promotions in the long term.

The problem is of course that "good enough" is just that. Mediocre. Getting by. If two people put in the same amount of time, but one does what is necessary to be the best, one will be promoted and the other will still be an assistant.

STILL GETTING TESTS

Most people think when they finish school, they had seen the last of tests, grades, pop quizzes, and final exams. Unfortunately, this is not true. Each contact you have with your GM is a pop quiz. Every question asked of you is a test, and every shift is graded.

In school, a student could bring up his/her grade point average the next semester by studying more. In business, it doesn't happen that way. There is no making up grades, no starting a new semester because the GM remembers all your grades. "C's" will not get you promoted. You want and need "A's". In business, "F" stands for fired.

BUT WHAT IF I SCREW UP?

First, if you do screw up, never, ever try to cover it up. Don't blame others, don't make excuses. Even though you have disappointed yourself and the GM, being honest will get it behind you faster. This will also get the GM to trust you. If you can be trusted to tell the truth with tough situations, you can be trusted for most everything.

Use your screw-ups to be learning experiences. When you screw up, attempt to figure out *why* you screwed up. What made you choose the path that you took? What were your assumptions and what were the actions and consequences that went through your mind when you were deciding? Go over them with your GM to fully understand how and why you made the wrong decision. The GM will appreciate you doing this. Trust me, very few assistant managers go to this trouble.

• Dependable. You are where you are supposed to be when you are supposed to be.

• Professional. Your appearance should be at least equal to the GM's.

• Knowledgeable. If you don't know, find out.

• Organized.

• Never procrastinate

OK. GOT IT. WORKING ON THEM. WHAT'S NEXT?

1. Know the GM's priorities.

Learn what your GM really cares about and make sure that is your priority. If you're not sure, ask the GM directly. When the GM says (or even suggests) that something needs to be done, do it. Now. Don't procrastinate. By taking care of anything your GM thinks is important immediately, you'll build the GM's confidence in you. Likewise, if you wait till the GM mentions the same task again, you are going to disappear as promotable.

2. Volunteer

To build your skills and to show you care about more than just yourself, volunteer. First, you'll probably learn something you don't know. Second, it shows that you are not too good to do some work that no one else wants. Third, it shows that you are not afraid of more responsibility, in fact you want it. To be promotable, you must want more responsibility and must want to get better. To do both, you must get out of your comfort zone by doing things you've never done before. You'll get better and wonder why you were ever bothered before. This is tough at first, but worth it in the end.

3. Talk like your GM.

Remember your accounting classes? No? That's ok but read or reread the chapter on numbers. To have your GM think of you as promotable, you've got to talk like a GM. This means knowing the income statement backwards and forwards. If you are not yet comfortable using the terms of the income statement, make a point of learning it. Go down the P&L line by line. If you are uncertain about what any line means, go to the GM or other assistant manager for an explanation. The GM expects a promotable manager to be able to communicate by using the jargon, words, and phrases of the income statement.

4. No surprises for the GM.

You want your GM to hear about any incidents that happened on your shift from you first, even if the incident seemed small at the time. If there is even the slightest chance that an incident might later be brought to the GM, leave detailed notes on the situation and how you handled it, plus any witnesses who were there. You want to avoid any surprises for the GM.

For example, a customer falls, and when you go over and ask how he is, the customer says fine, no problem. Even though the customer said all is well, make notes covering the time, date, your knowledge of the incident, what the customer said, and what you said. Often, the customer will go home, find that they are in pain, and go to the doctor. Or sometimes they file an accident claim much later. However small an incident may seem and whatever the reason, write it up. This is one time when TMI is a good thing.

5. Figure out what behaviors the GM likes and dislikes.

Be aware of your GM's hot buttons, things that if you do them (or don't do them) could trigger a serious meltdown.

6. Whenever possible, get to know the GM on a personal level

One of the keys to a good work relationship is connecting on a personal level. This can be tougher than it sounds because you don't want to ask too many personal questions and you don't want to share too many details about your life too soon either. Ask basic questions at first and let the GM take the lead on how much you should ask or tell. You want to come across as curious and respectful, not prying or sucking up.

7. Ask for Advice

Believe it or not, you look stronger, not weaker when you ask for advice. Don't do this to suck up, but only when you really want to have something explained.

8. Solve problems on your own

Instead of running to the GM for every problem that comes up, handle it yourself. Few GM's like to be bothered when you could handle it yourself. But, when you are unclear about what you are supposed to do or whether you have the authority to do something, absolutely ask. Handling problems by yourself and thinking through what you must do is a great way to grow and develop. Remember, you can't get better by doing the same things. You must be uncomfortable to grow.

HOW CAN I SUPPORT THE GM?

Look for ways to make your GM's job easier. What does your GM hate to do? What does the GM not do well? These are all great opportunities for you.

For example, I had a GM who hated to place orders. He would bitch about doing it each and every time. So, whenever I worked a shift directly before or after the GM, I placed the orders for him. I didn't make a big deal about it, just mentioned in the notes if it was a dinner shift or mentioned it to him in passing during the day. It was not a big deal for me to do this and didn't take much time, but I know the GM noticed and appreciated the extra effort.

Whenever possible be proactive. If you see something that needs doing, do it. You don't have to ask for permission for everything. Don't make a big deal that you did something extra, just make a note. Don't worry, it will be noticed. You're trying to be someone who does not need to be managed. When the GM can consistently rely on you, your reputation will grow.

Show the GM you care about becoming a better manager by taking advantage of the GM.

Whenever you make a decision that wasn't good, take the time to self-evaluate your decision. Go to the GM to go over your decision process in detail together so that you can identify where your assumptions were wrong. This will go a long way in showing the GM that you want to learn from your mistakes. Being proactive and self-sufficient allows the GM to see you as a peer, rather than as an employee who needs to be managed.

Pay attention. Be aware.

Observe how the GM operates, how the GM handles employee, and customer interactions. After a while you'll see what the GM values. Those are exactly what you need to focus on.

Go above and beyond

Remember, you can be the hardest working manager in the history of the world, work every hour in the week, but if you are not meeting budget and excelling every shift you're not going to get any respect. If you want the respect of your GM, the first step is to go a little above and beyond what is expected of you.

1. Do what you say you'll do when you said you would do it. Your GM must come to rely on you as their go-to person. This will bring more responsibility and trust that will lead to your promotion.

2. Take responsibility vs. make excuses. Sometimes, of course, you will screw something up. When this happens, take full responsibility.

3. Come with solutions, not complaints or gripes. When you have a complaint about anything and you need to go to the GM about it, make sure you have a solution in mind. If you just cannot come up with a solution, at least go over the steps you took to try.

The value of a good relationship is that it gives you a solid foundation when your costs are out of line or stressful times arise. Without that relationship, you won't have the open communication and sense of trust needed to resolve issues quickly. Instead, you should have a strategic plan to "manage up" and figure out how to work with your manager more effectively.

HERE ARE A FEW MORE THINGS TO HELP MANAGE UP.

1. Do Your Job Well

Your number 1 priority. The best way to manage up is to do your job well. Keep focused on top performance. Most people do desire a good relationship with their boss, but if you don't have one, invest the time and energy you have into doing the best job you can do.

2. If the GM thinks it's important, you do too.

Your job is to support your GM. Focus on any issue the GM thinks is important.

3. Develop a Positive Relationship

If you think about it, you spend more time with your managers than with nearly any other person in your life. Yet so many people leave this relationship to chance or neglect it completely. Instead, make the effort to get to know your manager as a person.

4. Understand the GM's Goals

If you aren't clear on those things, now's the time to set up a one-on-one meeting to fix that. Why? Because everything you do is directly tied to that. By understanding his or her goals, you'll be able to see how your work ties into the group's success and see how your day-to-day responsibilities are part of the bigger picture.

5. Anticipate the GM's Needs

Once you understand your boss' goals, you'll be better equipped to anticipate his or her needs.

6. Don't continually bug the GM

Don't assume that you can just bother the GM whenever you have the smallest question. The GM will probably be patient for a while, but not forever. Learn the most opportune times to ask questions so that the GM can focus on you. Always attend every meeting, return every phone call, and answer emails as soon as possible.

7. Under-Promise and Over-Deliver

If your GM feels like she needs to continually check in with you it means the GM is worried about you, this is a problem. Keep your commitments. Keep your GM in the loop about the progress you're making before she asks.

8. Do not procrastinate

This is often tough for new managers because they are sometimes used to waiting till the last minute to start. Procrastination always creates anxiety when something is due, but not ready. Force yourself to get your tasks done, even the smallest tasks, as soon as you can. Starting early allows you time to ask questions if needed or to easily fix something that could be giant problems close to the deadline. Remember, things always get screwed up when you are in a time bind. The internet goes down, the guy you needed to see is on vacation, your printer decides now is the time to not work. Can you say stress? Completing work ahead of time earns cred from your GM. The GM must trust that you will do what you say you're going to do. On time is good. Early is better. Late is a deal breaker.

OH NO, YOU DISAGREE!

There will, of course, be times when you disagree with your GM, and that's OK if you do it in a respectful way. Ask for the reasons that back up the decision. Make sure you have reasons that you put forth. Your GM will respect that you have strong opinions, but only if you have solid reasons to back it up. WARNING: Once the GM decides, drop it. Your job is now to support the GM.

DOUBLE WARNING: Do not ever say to employees that you disagree with the GM. This will undermine you with the employees and when the GM hears (and he will) that you told employees that you don't agree with the GM, you are toast.

UNDERSTAND YOUR MANAGER'S STYLE

One key to managing up at work is to get to know your GM's management style.

- Do they prefer that you check with them before making even minor decisions or do they give you independence in making decisions?
- Do they prefer to communicate via email, one on one meetings, or wait till a meeting?
- How often do they want your updates—daily, weekly, or only when asked?

Once you understand how your manager manages, you can adapt to your boss's communication and decision-making style. The more you can match your GM when communicating, the more they will really hear what you are saying.

The more you can anticipate problems as well as your manager's needs, the more confidence and influence you build. This approach makes a welcome impression and shows that you are proactive. If you know that bad news is coming, tell the GM as soon as possible. The worst possible scenario is that your manager is the last to know. Take the initiative so that they can be prepared and of course, keep a good attitude.

> *If you just must vent, go in the walk-in*
> *and yell at the carrots.*

When at work, stay upbeat and engaged. Never bad-mouth your GM. You never know who is watching or listening. They always find out and it will not go well.

Do just a bit more than expected.

No need to go nuts, but if, for example, the GM asks you to organize the storeroom, make sure you also redo labels and put the storeroom in either inventory order or vendor order. It's a way to provide a bit more than expected. Do more than expected each time you have a task or project.

You don't have to be the ultimate, greatest, most wonderful assistant manager. Think about baseball or football coaches. Few, if any coaches were superstars when they played. When your GM knows that you understand the total picture, trusts your judgments, and feels confident that you could run the restaurant, you are ready for promotion. A great way to earn trust is when the GM is not around, such as on vacation. Another way and a much more powerful way is when YOU are not around. How do your employees in your area respond when you are not there? If your employees are still excellent when you are not around, it reflects good management.

WHAT WOULD YOU DO?

You have just finished your management training, and you are now the assistant manager in charge of the dining room--servers, bussers, and door hosts/hostesses.

Your GM tells you to shape up the dining room. The GM says that there are many problems, and he expects you to solve them.

Here are the problems: Many complaints about the service from the customers. Many complaints from the servers about the hosts/hostesses. The servers say that they either get seated all at once or only rarely get seated. The hosts say that the servers come up to the hostess stand and harass them, yelling at them when they are not seated. Both the servers and the hosts complain that the bussers are not bussing quickly enough. The bussers complain that they are slow because the servers never prebus. It is chaos, with everyone blaming someone else.

What would you do?

WHAT I DID

- I organized a focus group that included a busser, host, and server.
- I held it away from the restaurant at a nearby pizza place where we could sit together and talk.

REFLECTION

I am a big believer in focus groups. They have always worked out well, solving problems, bonding unlikely groups of employees and having a built-in group to help in selling it to the other employees to ensure it works.

SUGGESTIONS FOR SUCCESSFUL FOCUS GROUPS

In a focus group, you are the facilitator. Invite a representative from every position that has skin in the game. Make it a big deal. Recruit them by telling them you're organizing a select group to help in solving a problem in the restaurant. Make sure you only invite employees who are well respected and influential, but each must be eager to join in and help.

Once you have the group, invite them to dinner at a place where you can get together and talk without disturbing other customers. After getting settled, thank them for joining. Tell them the problem, then ask each person to give their perspective of the problem. After that, ask the group for solutions. Be open, don't slam any of the suggestions, but if any won't work, tell them why.

My experience has been that the employees who accepted being in the focus group always felt very energized and always bonded together. They felt very motivated to solve whatever problem I introduced.

More importantly, they would usually come up with great solutions to solve the problem. One huge benefit is that each member of the focus group worked hard to persuade their friends to go along with the suggestions helping you tremendously.

> **WARNING:** It is essential that you keep the focus group informed and give them feedback about what the GM and other managers thought. Be sure to let the group know if any of the suggestions that the focus group recommended will be implemented.

If you don't keep them informed, this whole focus group concept will go down in flames and instead of a very positive, prestigious group, it will be a joke.

PART 3

Danger
Zone

CHAPTER 8

CAREER KILLERS AND HOW TO AVOID THEM

*Nobody appreciates what I do
until I don't do it*

I n an ideal world, we have ideal bosses who coach, support, and mentor. Mistakes are allowed because they can be great learning experiences. Our general manager will take us aside in private to make us aware of mistakes, patiently walk us through why they were bad decisions, and advise us to consider alternatives on what we could have done with the pros and cons of each. All that's left for us to do is not make the same mistake twice.

Unfortunately, reality is seldom ideal. In the real world, these common mistakes could cost you your job or slow your career to a crawl.

To give you a competitive edge, here are the most common mistakes that I have seen many new managers make and how to avoid them.

HAVING A RELATIONSHIP WITH AN EMPLOYEE

Big, Giant, Flashing Red No-No. I saw this happen twice in my career and both times it ended badly. It is easy to understand how getting into a relationship with an employee happens--your employees are close to your own age, they're attractive, and energetic. Mix in late nights and alcohol and you have a highly combustible mixture.

There are only two outcomes that can happen when a manager gets into a relationship with an employee.

A. They fall in love, get married and live happily ever after.

Never happens. OK, it does happen, but rarely.

B. The relationship ends. Things get bad (really bad) between the manager and the employee usually ending or jeopardizing the manager's career.

First things first.

You may think that no one will find out about the relationship.

Wrong.

Everyone knows.

NOTHING is secret in a restaurant. Nothing.

If you've worked in a restaurant for more than a day, you quickly realize that there are no secrets in a restaurant. Every one of your employees knows that you, the manager, are in a relationship with an employee.

When a relationship between a manager and an employee develops, other employees won't care at all while others will care a great deal. But every employee will be looking to see if you play favorites. Most likely you are doing all you can to appear disinterested in the employee, maybe even hostile, but everyone knows about your "secret".

Inevitably, one of you will want the relationship to end. Regardless of the reason, there comes a point in the relationship when one of you regrets the relationship and wants it over.

If the employee feels wronged, the employee often will seek to punish the manager by sending an email or telling the GM or the district manager about the affair between you and an employee. This gets very ugly, and you, my friend, are officially toast which is never good for your career. This will be miserable for everyone. Morale goes down. Employees choose sides. You, the manager, will always lose.

Sometimes the manager gets a really, really stupid idea to simply get rid of the 'problem' employee". The manager looks for ways to fire the employee or get the employee to quit. Minor disciplinary write ups are given, bad schedules are handed out, and bad stations are assigned to the employee. This will prove to be one of this manager's worst ideas. When this starts to happen, you can bet that the employee will immediately call or email the district manager or GM to tell him the "secret" of the affair with the employee. This is the perfect way to set yourself and your company up for a sexual harassment lawsuit.

Think about how this would play at an employment relations board hearing-- "Sir, the manager threatened to fire me if I didn't sleep with him. I'm a single mother and I needed my job". Even if it was the most consensual relationship that has ever existed, who do you think an employment relations board will likely believe? The employee almost always wins.

How to avoid:

• Don't put yourself in a position that may compromise yourself.

• If you suspect an employee likes you in a relationship kind of way, make sure to always have other employees around.

• I strongly suggest that you never go to an employee's apartment. Just say that as a personal policy, you don't go to any employee homes. They'll understand and respect what you say.

• Resist the temptation to meet employees at a bar for drinks after a shift. I wouldn't go even if it is in a large group. Too many negative things can happen which outweighs any good. There is nothing wrong with keeping some distance with your employees.

• Avoid being the last manager in the restaurant with the one employee that you are even a little bit interested in or who might be interested in you.

• If you find yourself really, really caring about an employee at your restaurant, there is a simple and professional way to handle it. One of you either transfers or gets another job. Problem solved.

BEING TOO TOUGH / TOO SOFT ON YOUR EMPLOYEES

It is normal for new managers to begin their management careers by being either too tough on employees or too soft on employees. Managers who are naturally nice, trusting, and naive usually start at the soft end. Some may have heard that it is always best to start off too hard, because you can always dial it down, but if you start off too soft, it is more difficult to get tougher, so you come in hard with guns blazing.

Let's call this your management style. We're all different with different backgrounds. Some of us tend to be more understanding and others tend to be more rigid. But whichever style you have, look at the line below. Minus 5 would be extremely soft towards employees while plus 5 would be extremely hard on employees. Where would you put yourself on this line and where on the line do you think is best?

Soft -5 -4 -3 -2 -1 0 +1 +2 +3 +4 +5 Hard

I've done this exercise a hundred times in management workshops and in restaurant management classes. After asking each manager or student where they are on the line above, inevitably just about every point is covered, with most between the -2 and +2, and others all over.

It has been my experience that new managers, regardless of which end they start at, will get burned by their employees. What usually happens is that the hard managers will come down unreasonably hard on their employees, which makes the employees resent these managers causing a bad attitude which they will find ways to get back at the manager. The same holds true for the "soft" managers, just in a different way. Employees will take advantage of the soft managers by not doing anything that the soft manager asks them to do, such as required side work or closing duties. When asked by the manager if they had done the required work, they assure the manager that they have. But, when the manager checks on them, they have not done their duties. This means that the manager now gets to do it himself or, if he didn't bother to check, the manager who follows this manager will see what was not done. Not good.

After the new manager realizes that he is not having success from his management style, the tendency is to swing drastically to the opposite side. The soft manager becomes hard and the hard manager becomes soft. It will be painfully obvious that neither style fits every situation.

Ways to avoid:

• The promotable manager realizes that there is no one best way. Think of each point on the line (-5 to +5) as a tool in your toolbox. You want to use the tool that fits the situation and one size definitely does not fit all.

• The 'best' way to treat employees is to treat each employee as an individual. When you are stuck with only one management style for everyone, it works for no one.

• Ideally, you want to be able to use every one of the points on the line from the very softest to the very hardest, depending on who you are speaking with and the situation. When you speak to a very good employee, be soft. All you have to do is ask this type of employee and he'll do it willingly. But, if you were to tell him ("Do it, or I'll fire you"), he will resent it and after a while, develop a bad attitude and maybe even quit. But the opposite is also true. If you have an employee who is a problem, the best approach is not to ask, but to tell. Sometimes the hard way is the right way, and you can't be afraid or tentative to use it. It is difficult to go outside your comfort zone in management style but force yourself. You will be a much more effective manager.

• To better develop your entire range, one suggestion is to take the Enneagram personality test. This is available online and in workshops and there are many books on the subject.

Different styles for different situations. Kind of like working around the house, you wouldn't want to only have a hammer. Might need pliers too.

OK IS NOT GOOD ENOUGH.

Many new managers don't really know what their standards are, especially when coming into restaurant management for the first time. They often look to other assistant managers or their general manager to define their standards. This may seem logical and practical, but beware. It is essential that if your fellow managers (including your GM) have standards that are less than yours (without being perfectionist, see Perfectionist in this list), that you hold true to your own standards. Standards come into play often during a shift; in handing out discipline, how your employees answer the phone, to standards of cleanliness or how you complete a task.

The importance of standards was brought home to me when I was an assistant manager tasked to do a simple job. All I had to do was redo the employee bulletin board. The bulletin board was basically just a bunch of employee schedules pinned to the corkboard with other notices and random notes. All I had to do was organize it, get it neat, and that was it. Simple.

So, I hand drew titles for the different categories (Server schedule, Kitchen schedule, etc.) and then pinned the schedules under them. Done. When I told my GM that I had finished the bulletin board, he came to see. I could immediately tell that all was not good.

Then he did something I would always be thankful for. He stood back and asked me to tell him how well he thought I had done. I was surprised when I looked at the completed bulletin board through his eyes.

After a minute, I was shocked to see how really terrible a job I had done. The titles were crooked and sloppy since I had just hand drawn them and not typed. **I had treated this job as a task to just get it done.** This simple lesson by my GM got me to appreciate a job done well. It really is what separates the best managers from mediocre managers.

TRAP

New managers can be tempted to avoid hassles by not dealing with employees who are not working up to standards. This is especially true when new managers are non-confrontational by nature or lack confidence. After all, it is a hassle to point out a problem to an employee, then have to coach them on the correct way, or have to do a write up. It would be so easy just to not notice the problem in the first place. This is especially true towards the end of a shift when everyone is tired. The problem with this is that employees notice which of the managers keep their standards and which do not. **Your employees will live up (or down) to the standards set by each manager**.

WARNING: When employees call the restaurant to see which manager is working a particular shift usually means that they want to know if they have to bring their A game or whether their B game is good enough.

How to avoid:

- Keep true to yourself, tempering your standards with common sense.

- Keep your standards consistently high, even if is a hassle occasionally. Most of your employees will welcome your standards because it leads to smooth shifts, higher tips, and less stress.

- Treat even the simplest task as a quality job, not something just to complete and check off. Do each task   as well as you possibly can. Any time you finish a task, take a minute to take a cold, hard, objective look at it. Is this the best you can do? GM's notice which assistants consistently do a great job.

NOT BEING SERIOUS AT WORK

Over the years, I have had several good assistant managers who had a really tough time getting promoted. They were all good natured, optimistic, and very nice people, good technically and worked hard, but each had a common fatal flaw that kept holding them back: each gave off the impression that they didn't take their job seriously. They told too many jokes, talked too much with employees about trivial matters, and tried too hard to get employees to like them. These actions leave the perception that a manager does not take their job seriously. Maybe being the life of the party worked in college or while an employee, but this does not fly in management. Even worse, the general manager can assume, fairly or not, that they probably are too close to their employees, have low standards, should be paying more attention, and that employees run all over them.

Any time you come across as too casual, a promotion is just not going to happen. It is impossible to entrust a multi-million-dollar operation to someone who does not take their job seriously. Obviously, occasionally telling jokes or talking with your employees is not bad, but only when done in moderation. If you suspect this may be holding you back, changes need to occur. Once you have gotten the reputation that you are too casual, it is very difficult to undo.

How to avoid:

• Tone it down. Recognize when you are starting to get off focus or hanging with a particular employee too much.

• Make a checklist for each shift, including your daily and weekly goals, that keep you focused on your priorities.

• Be aware when you start to kid around at work. Remember, you are in a business situation where the expectation is that you are focused on work.

• If you suspect that you have this perception, go speak to your GM. Ask for a very candid appraisal. Ask specifically if he has a problem with taking you seriously. This might require just a few relatively painless changes to take place to get the early perception to change.

AVOIDING CUSTOMERS

All too often, new managers are petrified when they must speak or interact with customers, especially if they perceive there is a problem waiting for them. When they get even a hint of a customer problem, they sometimes find something urgent that requires their immediate attention, usually in the office or deep in the kitchen. Every one of your employees know which managers they can rely on to help with problem customers and they know which managers are afraid of customers. One day, one of them will tell your general manager. It is best for your career and your well-being to get over this. Here's how.

How to avoid:

• You have the power to fix just about any problem. Realize that most customers are delighted and pleasantly surprised to see a manager. Most simply want to talk about a problem and all you must do is listen. Others expect you to do something and you can and should do something.

• Talk with your GM about what you can and cannot do for customers. Make sure you come away knowing your powers and limitations that your GM sets in taking care of customer problems. You should feel much more prepared to deal with customers since you'll know what you can and can't do.

• Force yourself to speak with customers. When I first started in restaurant management, I hated talking with customers. I got over this by telling each of my servers that when any of their customers had even a hint of dissatisfaction, to let me know and I would go over and talk with them. After a while, I overcame my fear of customers, actually came to enjoy the interactions, and looked forward to that part of my shift.

• To help get you started, notice a specific item that they are eating and ask about it. Don't just ask how their meal is/was. Then maybe, ask about them: how far do they have to drive to the restaurant? How often do they come in? Do they have a favorite server? Why? What is their favorite meal? Then you can ask if they have any suggestions that may help the restaurant to be better. They'll love it.

• Give each "problem" customer your business card. Giving them your business card will show them that you are sincere that you'd like to talk with them again. Tell them that the next time they're in, to ask their server if you're in and if you are, you'd love to personally make sure they are being taken care of.

• Go to problem customers. Tell your servers that if they

sense that they have a customer who is unhappy, you'd like to talk with them. Your employees appreciate and love you for this. Go to the customers with the attitude that whatever is wrong, you can make them want to come back. You don't have to give away free meals, appetizers, or drinks every time either. In most cases, the customers just want to vent. Don't be surprised if your "problem" customers turn out to be your most loyal customers who you look forward to seeing the next time they come in.

LAPSE OF INTEGRITY

It is tragic when a manager is fired for cheating. Most involved covering up some problem in their area of responsibility, such as high food cost, high labor cost, or some other problem related to an assistant's responsibility. So, the manager cheats on inventories, goes short staffed to help labor percentage, or takes shortcuts. There is also temptation in a restaurant to steal, especially for managers. After all, this is a cash intensive business with plenty of opportunities to take cash, food, wine, liquor, and supplies, most of which can be used at home. I've seen managers who would take a $20 bill and mark it as a receipt in petty cash or just put as 'cash under' in the deposit. Easy to do, but wrong. Eventually, you'll get caught.

How to avoid:

If being a good person with high integrity isn't enough, then think of the consequences. It will destroy your career, reputation, relationships, and self-esteem and follow you professionally for a very long while. Think of the Nike ad in reverse: Just don't do it.

PLAYING FAVORITES

This is a no brainer, but it is difficult to avoid because some employees are, well, your favorites and you want to take care of the employees who are your favorites. Usually, they are your favorites because they are excellent employees.

Sometimes though, even the best employees will try to play you. They will suck up to you because they think you can help them, such as their schedules. Playing favorites always gets noticed by employees and causes massive amounts of resentment. Keep in mind that not one employee will resent you for being fair to everyone.

How to avoid:

- Have objective ways to measure the best employees.

- Treat everyone fairly and consistently.

- Be aware when you tend to be friendlier with only a select few employees

BEING TOO CLOSE TO YOUR EMPLOYEES

Similar to Playing Favorites, but different. The problem shows up when those "favorite" employees gradually start crossing the line between employee/employer relationship into taking advantage of your relationship. This is something that will be so gradual that you might notice, but choose to ignore, because you will think it is a onetime thing. It won't be. Keep some distance between yourself and your employees. This is dangerous because it can put you in an awkward situation eventually when you must discipline them.

How to avoid:

- Do not meet with employees after work for a drink or dinner.

- Do not go to employee's apartments.

- Be alert for employees getting too familiar with you.

SPENDING TOO MUCH TIME AT WORK

Although the restaurant industry gets criticized (often deserved) about the amount of time managers work, every single profession requires more than 40 hours per week to get ahead. Virtually all management and professional positions (Lawyers, doctors, engineers) require working way more than the 40 hours per week.

But there is a point when enough is enough. Better scheduling can prevent managers from working back to back shifts (a close shift followed by an open shift). Sometimes it is managers, especially new managers, thinking they need plenty of "face time", so they wait to leave after their GM leaves and arrive before the GM. Sometimes it is that they fear that there will be problems with their area of responsibility unless they are there, so they come in early and stay way too long (this is covered in another chapter in detail).

How to avoid:

• When your shift is over, don't hang around, leave by the nearest exit door. However, before you leave, take two minutes to ask the incoming manager if he/she needs anything. This is the proper thing to do and the professional thing to do. They will appreciate this just as you would when you take over a shift from them. Then leave. Now. It is so easy to take care of just one more thing. In a foodservice operation, there is always one more thing. Just leave.

• Talk with the GM about what a complete shift looks like. What are the GM's expectations that a manager must complete before leaving? Don't assume.

• Unfortunately, there are some GM's who do expect their assistants to arrive before them and stay late. Ask the other assistants what they think is expected. When the GM is following you on a shift, when you are ready to leave, go to the GM and tell him what you've done to help (for an example, placed an order that the

GM would have to do) and ask him if there is anything that you can do before you leave. When he says everything is ok, leave. On a jet plane. Get out of there.

TOO PERFECTIONIST

Many really good assistant managers start off as perfectionists only to find that the restaurant business usually chews up perfectionists. That's because while the perfectionist is making sure each detail is perfect, taking time and effort, the other parts of the restaurant could be going to hell. An effective manager must be able to be all over the restaurant without staying at one place too long. Whether you are female or male, being perfectionistic hurts because it often makes for spending way too much time on something that is "good enough". If you find yourself taking loads of time making sure that something is absolutely, positively right, then you are probably spending too much time. But look at your General Manager. What standard does the GM require? If you're really not sure, ask. He may say that you are spending way too much time on perfection while ignoring other, equally important duties. You don't want this stigma since it takes so long to get rid of the perception.

How to avoid:

• Don't allow yourself to get bogged down in one area, especially when the restaurant is open and running. When things get chaotic (and they will), the 80-20 rule is good to follow. As things calm down, you can drill down into more specific.

NOT DETAIL ORIENTED

This can be very frustrating for the GM. This was one of my problems that I had to fight. Often, after a shift, my GM would let me know that I had missed doing something on my shift. Usually something small, and usually a different something on each shift. If this had happened once, no problem. But when you miss something each shift, there's a problem.

How to avoid:

• I always found that having a checklist for everything made all the difference. I had a different checklist for when I was closing manager, opening manager, ordering, inventory, anything, and everything. This forced me to do everything required while not missing anything. Many restaurant chains have very good checklists that they encourage managers to use.

• Make sure you go over each checklist before you actually have to use them, so you understand what each step means, and you know how to do each one of them.

• Don't be afraid to customize your checklist to make it really work for you. Add steps to the checklist that fit you better.

NOT JUMPING ON PROFIT & LOSS PROBLEMS

This is the big kahuna, and it is discussed fully in its very own chapter. Most new managers realize that they must have good budget numbers and that they must take action when they are over budget. The problem is that some assistants do not take a proactive approach as soon as a problem presents itself. Every manager will have budget problems, but it is the promotable assistant who acts immediately or better yet, works to prevent the problems from happening in the first place.

How to avoid:

See chapter on Budgets and Profit & Loss (P&L). Anticipate your problem P&L areas. Have an action plan to bring it in line as soon as possible and then work the plan.

PROCRASTINATE

If there is one thing that will ruin your reputation it is being overdue with schedules, orders, or anything. When you commit to doing something by a certain date and time, make sure it happens. Do it early, not later. One reason is that if you have problems early, you can always start over or ask for help. However, if you run into problems when it is due tomorrow, you're screwed. If you ask for help, it may be too late to salvage, and everyone will know you procrastinated. Of course, if you don't ask for help, you're even more screwed.

I realize that this is one of the most difficult personal habits to get rid of (ask me how I know). It might be because you've always been able to pull it off at the last minute or you didn't suffer any consequences if you were late, so you never learned to stop procrastinating. At first, you'll probably have to force yourself to work on something but do force yourself. It might not get any easier, but at least you'll get the discipline needed to get everything done on time.

Be early, every time, for every project, for every shift, for every schedule. It is vital that you are dependable in every area of management.

DISORGANIZED

I was casual about this at first. But this was driven home to me how serious I should take it when I was asked by my supervisor to give him a ride to the airport. When we got in my car, I realized that it was a disaster, with newspapers, magazines, and cups littering the back seat. I was so embarrassed, but it was too late. I realized right then that just about everything, including my car, goes into making your perception at work.

How to avoid:

• Take an extra minute to keep your car, office, and yourself organized. You just never know when someone that matters will see.

• Do whatever it takes to be early or on time, every time. If it takes you 30 minutes to get to work, leave 45 minutes early.

• Don't wait to do a project or task the day before it is due because something will usually happen to prevent you from completing it on time. This happened to me when I had dedicated the day before my schedule was due to complete it when I got a call that one of the other managers had an emergency and I had to cover his shift. This meant of course, that I would be late with my schedule. I had no excuse. I had to work on the schedule when I got home again. Working on my schedule at the end of a long shift cured me of procrastinating. Remember, this is your career. Your GM files that away and it will take you a longgggg time to regain his confidence.

NOT TAKING CARE OF YOUR AREA

This is a trap. Most new managers (and most people in general) gravitate to doing things they like to do. Be careful of this. Often the problem is minor, but the new manager enjoys this type of problem, such as a small software problem in the POS system. The new manager will spend hours tracking down the cause of the glitch when he should be using that time on his own specific area. Unless your General Manager has specifically asked you to work on a problem outside of your area, don't spend your time. The only exception would be if you are totally on top of your own area. But be careful, if your area declines because you worked on someone else's area, it will not be good. Focus, young Jedi.

How to avoid:

- Only get involved in other things after your own area is taken care of. Do not volunteer your time when you need to spend that time on your own area.

- Your area is your priority.

NOT BEING A TEAM PLAYER

Your restaurant is one team that you want to succeed. You want the restaurant to look good because when the restaurant looks good, everyone looks good. When your restaurant is recognized as one of the best, each assistant manager has a better chance of being recognized as one of the best. It's like a football team that wins the national championship. It is much easier for one of the assistant coaches to get promoted to head coach from a winning team than from a losing team. If the GM thinks that one manager could help another and does not, that manager's reputation will suffer.

How to avoid:

If you can help a fellow manager, help. This is not the place to have a win-lose attitude. You want the restaurant to look as good as it can and that means looking after your fellow managers. (But see Not Taking Care of Your Area above).

ARGUING WITH THE GM

Sometimes new managers can have a false sense of entitlement, have too strong an ego, or are overconfident and really believe that they know better than the GM. Chances are you don't, especially if you're new to restaurant management.

Sometimes, what may look simple and straight forward to you just might turn out to be complex or you are missing something.

Or the GM just doesn't want to hear any negatives period. While it is helpful and healthy to have discussions that question why a decision was made as a way to learn, it is decidedly unhealthy for your career if A) you push back with questions or negativity all the time, B) keep pushing back after the GM has hinted or said that the issue has been decided, C) suggest that you are right and your GM is wrong, but maybe the worst is D) to have a bad attitude after the GM has made a decision that you don't agree with. If you go away with a negative attitude, you will seldom support the decision 100%. Your employees will immediately pick up on this and know you don't really mean it. To them this is a clear signal that you will not enforce the new decision which means they won't do it. This translates that any shift that you are on will not run like the GM wants it to. If the GM doesn't notice immediately, someone will tell the GM that when you are managing, the standards are not enforced. Once again not good.

How to avoid:

This is easy. Don't do it. This doesn't mean to just roll over every time the GM says something, but it does mean to be sensitive to the GM. Asking questions to clarify and to better understand is great, just recognize limits.

• Know your GM's tolerance for push back and don't go beyond that point. This should be easy to tell.

• Most important! Once a decision has been made, get on board with enthusiasm. No resentments. No half ass. When you get to be GM, you can do it your way. I guarantee you will expect your assistant managers to follow your lead with enthusiasm and good attitude.

BEING INCONSISTENT- AVOID UPS AND DOWNS

Being consistent is tough, no question about it. But consistency is essential for gaining the trust of your GM. When you commit to doing something, make sure   it is as good as done. When you're the opening manager, you're there before your employees to open the door. You're not 5 minutes late. You're early. Every time. You cannot be great for a while and then be mediocre for a while when you are obviously just going through the motions, with no enthusiasm and no energy. But the worst part of this is that you will also be lax in your standards overlooking most problems except the most major ones that you can't avoid. Your shift suffers, your employees suffer, the whole restaurant suffers, and of course, your reputation suffers.

Or you might have an argument with your partner or parent; might have a sick relative, might have money problems, might have a son or daughter who is driving you crazy, your car might break down, there are countless possibilities for you to have a bad attitude or just be drained of any energy. Most promotions and opportunities happen when you least expect it. Most average managers go through cycles of ups and downs, sometimes for good reasons too. But promotable managers keep their performance consistently good.

Opportunities always seem to come during the lows. Promotable managers always level these out so they are consistent, and always ready for the opportunity. Be at your best all the time, not just now and then. This requires daily focus and work on your part, but your career is worth it.

It is essential that you maintain a very steady, consistent work ethic and steady demeanor every single day. You absolutely do not want to become so casual that your manager has to jack you up for you to get better. Especially bad if this is a pattern. Your career could probably survive if this happened once, but not a second time.

It is written in stone that two things always go together--downward trends and opportunities. When you downward trend starts that is inevitably when the great opportunity to be promoted appears and guess what? You will not be chosen be-cause you're not ready. It is essential that you always have a good day, work hard, and that you're always "on". Don't relax your stan-dards, even when you're having a "bad day". Once again, no one will trust you to manage a multimillion-dollar operation over other managers and employees if your GM thinks you must be prodded or reprimanded to stay focused.

How to avoid:

Force yourself to be consistent. This was a problem of mine and the way I worked around this was to have a checklist for ev-erything. Nothing was left to chance because chance will usually let you down. With a checklist, you won't forget to lock the door, place an order, or do a line check ever again. Consistent.

SAYING YOU'RE JUST NOT GOOD AT SOMETHING

This is kind of like a new husband not doing a good job when his wife asks him to do the laundry in the hopes of getting out of doing it. This works with some wives ("if you want the job done right, I'll just have to do it myself"). But not with others. (I know). It is amazing that many new managers will actually say this to their GM when the GM asks (tells) them to do something. If you don't know how to do something, consider it a part of getting better and being a more complete manager. Treat it as learning one more skill that will make you one step closer to being pro-motable. I bet that many new managers know how to play the guitar or how to use a particular software program. I'll also bet they weren't good at it the first time they picked up the guitar or opened that software program. The reason you hung in there to learn it is because you wanted to because you thought the effort was worth the result. Treat this just like the guitar. Your career is worth the effort and your GM will appreciate your positive attitude. Remember that you can't grow without making yourself uncomfortable. You'll be surprised at how much more you enjoy your work when you know all aspects. And remember this takes you one step closer to promotion.

How to avoid:

Get good at it even if you don't like it.

BRINGING PERSONAL PROBLEMS INTO WORK

Everyone has the occasional personal problem, but we've all known people who seem to have more than their share of personal problems. Every day brings a new problem, a new crisis, or a rehashing of an old problem that they've talked about before. Many times before. When there are personal problems at home, problems with the spouse, significant other, parents or the dog, it is easy to bring this to work. When an assistant manager has a lot of personal problems, that person is not promotable. No one will risk promoting a manager into managing other managers and employees when they can't even manage themselves. It is obvious that these managers are distracted and not focused on their work.

How to avoid.

Everyone has bad days, and everyone has problems at home. The big difference is promotable managers don't have daily drama or daily personal problems. When they do have problems, they solve without bringing it into the restaurant. The restaurant is not the place to talk about them. If personal problems are serious, seek professional counseling. Often problems have been ignored or just haven't been dealt with. Take a long, hard, honest look, write them down, then figure out what can be done to solve them. Don't just put a band aid on them. It is always tempting for new managers to avoid dealing with unpleasant things, especially when it comes to personal problems, but you will find that taking care of problems when they happen results in a vast reduction of stress.

Whatever you do, leave personal problems at home; don't bring them to your restaurant.

NOT DELEGATING

When you first become a manager, it is tempting to want to do everything yourself. Later, you still might not delegate because you don't want to share in the "glory" or give up some power or you don't think you have any employees that can be trusted.

Fair enough, up to a point.

Once you are comfortable with your responsibilities and know your employees, start delegating. You will be far more effective as a manager, be able to get more things done, and you will develop employees which will pay off big time for you in the future.

How to avoid

This is treated in more detail in Managing your Shift chapter.

NOT WELCOMING MORE RESPONSIBILITY

The assistant manager who tries to avoid new or additional responsibilities will never be promoted, yet it happens all the time. If you don't think you're ready for a new responsibility, tell your GM your concerns directly. Make sure you have a game plan to get fully up to speed such as working with another assistant manager or with the GM for a short while. The absolute worst thing you can do is give the perception, real or imagined, that you do not want more responsibility. It will be the kiss of death for your career.

How to avoid.

Welcome new responsibility with enthusiasm and positive attitude. New responsibilities mean you're growing in ability and means you're that much closer to promotion.

Usually, the GM knows when you are ready for new responsibilities, whether you believe it yourself or not. Embrace the new responsibility and make the most of it. Change and growth are hard, but necessary in preparing for promotion.

Remember, **you can't get better without getting uncomfortable**.

HAVING A TASK MENTALITY

Anytime you have a task to complete, make sure you do it well. Get rid of the mindset that this is just something you need to accomplish to check off. This is an easy trap to get into. For example, maybe you've been given the task to clean out the back dock or a storeroom. So, you sweep, mop, clean, and organize. But you didn't relabel or move things to get in the corners. It's very easy to see if you have just completed a task to just get it done and move on. I mean, you've got thousands of things to do, so good enough is good enough, right? Wrong.

When your GM checks it out, it will be obvious if you've done a great job or an OK job, meaning you did it, but didn't think it was important. Do it well. I've known GM's who loved to hide a $20 bill in a spot that you might miss if you didn't do a good job. If it is just OK, redo it until you're proud of it. Your GM will be able to tell if you care or not. Think about when you become a GM, you'll expect nothing less from your assistants. You want to trust your assistants without having to check their work.

NOTE- You build your credibility each day with each task. Get the reputation of doing everything well the first time. Not just OK. You'll see the results when you are promoted.

NOT HAVING A CAREER PLAN

This is so important that it has its own chapter. The promotable manager plans his or her future because their careers are just too important to be left to chance. Promotable managers take actions that are intentional, not random. Once you grasp the importance of the career plan, you will take charge of your career. What a difference it will make.

How to avoid.

Read the chapter "Career Plan".

HAVING BAD DAYS

It is human nature to have bad days, but consistency is key to promotion. So many good assistant managers have missed opportunities for promotion because they had bad days or even weeks mixed in with lots of great periods. What usually happens is you get complacent; just go through the motions without really concentrating on your goals and just get by each day. The problem is that this is noticed. This up and down cycle kills any chance for promotion. Regardless of what is happening at home, car trouble, or you're just being lazy, force yourself to stay positive and keep the energy level up each day. I have seen many very, very good assistant managers miss out on promotions because they were in the down part of the cycle. Avoid this self-defeating loop that can and will stall your career.

EFFORT DOES NOT EQUAL RESULTS

Don't be fooled into thinking you'll be forgiven for problems because you've worked massive amounts of hours. At the end of the day, it is always about results, not effort. It doesn't matter the number of hours you worked or the intense effort that you made. Focus on results. That's why this book is about working smarter, not longer and not harder. I've seen many assistant managers who worked long, long hours, sacrificing time with their family and friends because they needed to be at work. At the end of the day, they still got fired or criticized by their GM because they did not deliver results.

Don't let yourself get caught in the trap of thinking that working long hours will protect you from a bad P&L. This will only cause frustration and bring on a severe negative attitude. In place of that, suck it up, go to your GM and tell him that you need advice in controlling your area.

CAUTION:

Do not go to the GM until you have a plan of your own that you believe will solve whatever problem you've got. It may not be the best plan, but it should be a plan that is obvious that you put thought into.

WHAT WOULD YOU DO?

You're ready for the lunch shift and you have a problem: Out of the 8 servers that you normally have, each having 4 tables each, you've had 3 servers call off.

What would you do?

WHAT I DID

- I expanded the stations, so it looked like the restaurant was more staffed than it was by having the hostess spread out the customers so that they could mainly see other customers and not just a lot of empty tables.

- I kept everyone at their normal 4 table stations except for two very strong servers who I gave 5 tables with instructions to the host to not seat the 5th table until the server said he was ready.

- I called in an extra busser to assist servers with running food, filling waters, etc.

- Emphasized to everyone that if they need me, ask.

- I got myself prepared for a lousy shift.

PROS AND CONS

A. Give everyone 5 or 6 tables.
Pros and cons
Pro –Less wait, more customers taken care of
Con—High potential for bad service, frantic servers, all leading to customer complaints

B. Keep everyone on 4 tables
Pros and cons
Pro – Keep good service, servers stay calm and not frantic
Con—Customers see empty tables and complain about wait. Lowers sales.

QUESTION:

- Is this a fluke or does it happen more often than you realize?

SUGGESTIONS TO PREVENT IN THE FUTURE:

- Add an on-call server to the schedule.

- Review your write up policy on being late, no show, or no callBe consistent.

- Even with good excuses, good people who are chronically late are a real problem and are not as good as you think.

- Chains are not as strict as you may thinkmany, many policies and procedures are up to the GM.

Overheard:
"No, we don't have WiFi.
Talk to each other".

CHAPTER 9

THE BOSS TALK: WHEN THINGS AREN'T GOING WELL, IT'S TIME TO MEET WITH THE GM

"Cover me, I'm going in."

A man told his friend that his mule always obeyed his every command. But when the man yelled "gideup," the mule just stood there—until the man hit the mule on the nose. As the mule started to move the man's friend said, "Why'd you do that? I thought you said he obeyed every command?"

"He always does," the man answered. "But first you have to get his attention."

TO MOVE FORWARD, MEET WITH THE GM

When your career is not moving forward or you realize that the GM does not have a good perception of you, you've got to speak to your GM. You've got to find out what is going on. Delaying this talk never makes it better. The situation will not go away by beating yourself up or complaining to friends. Ignoring it only makes it worse, leading to even more stress. Suck it up and talk with your GM. The sooner you meet, the sooner you'll know where you really stand and whether there is a chance to do something about it or not. Either way, you'll know and since you know, you'll now know what you must do.

Many assistant managers just can't make themselves meet with the GM. They would rather avoid the confrontation and try to ignore the problem, hoping that it will get better. The good thing about this is that the problem is avoided and you can go on about your life. The bad thing with this, of course, is that you will continue to agonize and stress about it. It is far better to know how bad a problem is than to avoid it. At least you'll know if your career is still good or if you should start looking for another job. Either way, you'll know and can start planning. Without knowing, no plan is possible.

Your GM is the gatekeeper who can move your career ahead, so when you're having a problem, the only possible action is to get a meeting with your GM and find out. By pushing for this meeting, you will get his attention in a big way. You will send a clear message that something is not right, you want to know what is wrong, and you want to take care of it.

The most difficult part about this meeting is the stress that goes with the anticipation of the meeting. Most people hate confrontation, especially with someone who may be hostile and who happens to be your GM. It can be a terrifying moment; a moment perfectly natural to rationalize why you don't need the meeting, but one that is absolutely necessary. It will not get better without you doing something and that something is a meeting.

This meeting, however difficult, is necessary and crucial to reverse negative perceptions the GM may have of you; perceptions that may be slowing or stopping your career. The meeting is meant to let your GM know that 1) your job and career are important to you; 2) you recognize there is a problem; and 3) you are ready to act.

WARNING! This meeting will put you directly on the GM's radar. This meeting will either make your career or kill it. **Either way, things will never be the same with your GM.**

DO I REALLY NEED THE MEETING?

There are two situations that require this meeting with the GM:

1) The GM is openly hostile.
2) You have become invisible.

Both situations are handled the same way to change the GM's perception of you.

In the first situation, a meeting with the GM can help head off getting fired, while the second is meant to change the GM's perception of you. The goal is to get your GM to see you differently and to believe that you are committed to changing your performance.

HOSTILE GM

The situation is critical. Pressure has built, and your GM is openly hostile, getting worse each shift. In this scenario, you feel like you are walking on eggshells. You hate coming in to work because you know your GM will be looking for you to make a mistake. The situation can also cause you to be so defensive, so not wanting to make a mistake, that you are reluctant in making decisions, even small decisions, without first going to the GM, which has made your performance suffer even more. Because you are under such intense stress, you are sensitive to any comments at home, causing real problems. Even though you hate the thought of going to the GM, you finally realize that you have to. You'd rather know sooner, not later, if you need to look for another job.

In this situation, the best action is to meet it head on by getting a direct meeting with your GM. You can't continue to try to avoid the GM. One of you will eventually blow up, causing you to resign immediately or the GM to actively seek to get you fired.

I'M INVISIBLE

In this situation, no one pays you any attention. You probably don't feel you're about to get fired, but the feeling of being ignored is strong. Typical indications that you have become invisible at work include the following:

- Your GM never asks your opinion.

- You are never included in special meetings or projects.

- Your performance evaluations are just OK.

- Your GM is nice enough, but indifferent.

In both cases, you just cannot take it anymore. Confronting the GM seems less of a problem than just continuing the way it is going. The only thing left is to do is meet with the GM. At least you'll know exactly why the GM is behaving this way towards you.

Seeing the GM is a big deal, so before you do this, you've got to be prepared. This preparation allows you to go into the meeting with confidence. You're going to find out what the real problem is and will determine whether you resign and look for another job or stay and change the GM's perception of you.

RELAX

The first thing that you must do when preparing for the meeting is relax. You will feel better once the decision to have the meeting is made. It is almost always the fear of the unknown that causes stress. After this meeting you will know whether you will be with this company or not. Either the GM will give you a chance or you will know that you will part ways. The main thing is that you'll know. No more unknowns and no more stress.

Suggestion: If you do not believe in your company or you can or want to change, you should not spend any more emotional energy. Skip to the last chapter, "What's holding you back?".

HOW TO "GET IT OVER WITH".

"You wanted to see me? What's up?" the GM asks, not even looking up.

"Yes, do you have a minute? I'm sorry to bother you, but I've been thinking a lot lately that you don't think I'm doing a good job. I'd like you to help me make a plan to show you just how good I really am."

You spoke in a timid, apologetic voice and looked depressed. This meeting was doomed from the start. It probably ended with you agreeing that it would be best if you gave two weeks' notice.

What went wrong?

To start with, you came across as unprofessional and weak. You started the meeting by asking if he had a minute, causing the GM to not think that this meeting was not particularly important. Your GM listened but didn't have faith in your conviction to change because you sounded apologetic with no confidence. Worst of all, you asked the GM to come up with a plan to improve your own work performance instead of you coming up with a plan and presenting it to the GM. Remember, you're management and you've got to start thinking like a manager which means coming up with solutions.

This was the story of a manager who had fallen into disfavor with the GM. The first problem is delaying the meeting, but the next problem when you finally realized that the meeting had to happen, was that you just wanted to get it over with. This "get it over with" attitude caused the meeting to happen with a weak approach, no preparation, no plan, and no formal meeting. With preparation, the meeting might have ended very differently.

PREPARE

To prepare for your meeting with the GM,

Organize

Use the assessments you made in the previous chapter, "What's the Score? Evaluating Current Reality," to better understand your GM's perspective. The three most important factors are:

- Your accomplishments over the past period of time.

- Reasons why you believe your GM has a negative perception of you.

- Incidents that occurred that you believe reinforced or caused your GM's negative perception about you.

The first step is to place yourself in your GM's shoes. Take a long, hard look at why you believe your GM has a negative perception of you and the incidents that caused it to happen. Look at yourself objectively and coolly, with as much detachment as possible. Do you have a sense why your GM might think the way he does? Does your GM's negative perception appear to be based on your performance, your behavior, or your attitude? Have you been late? Have you forgotten to place orders? Had some sloppy openings or closes? Seem to be always in panic mode, putting out fires?

This information will allow you to address your GM's perceptions squarely---and in a detached way--without being defensive.

Plan

When preparing for the meeting, plan to address the problem in a direct manner, highlight your resolve to change, and present a plan to ensure that it takes place.

- Break your plan down into parts. How will the GM respond to each part?

- Where do you think the single greatest point of resistance will be? What can you do to overcome it without causing greater conflict?

- Why is this plan best for your GM and for your company?

- Write down your key thoughts. Bring these notes to the meeting--you will have the confidence of knowing that nothing will be left out.

Tip Anticipate your GM's reactions. Ask yourself questions that you would have the greatest difficulty answering. What are the hardest questions you could be asked?

GM: *Why have you done just average work?*

GM: *What has caused you to change*

GM: *Why were you late? Why did you forget to place orders? How are you going to not do these again?*

GM: *Why should I believe you?*

As you develop your plan, remember the following:

- There should be a sense of urgency

- This is a time for action, not discussion

- Your GM wants you to be accountable-- don't make him responsible for your improvement

- No tolerance for excuses, only results. No "well buts".

- Build regular feedback into your plan.

An effective conversation with the GM might go something like this:

"I know you're worried about my performance. I am, too. "I know that the incident in March where I had a sloppy close and in April when I was negative about the new service program that came down from corporate made you lose confidence in me, and I realize I have done just average work for the past several months."

"I have thought a lot about my job. I know I can do it and do it well. I would like to go over a plan that I think will help me to be an asset rather than a liability. I have developed a set of performance goals that I'd like to show you."

Continue with what you intend to do (include completion dates), and finish with why this plan will work. Your plan must include scheduled GM meeting dates.

I would recommend a short meeting every two weeks with your GM. More often than every two weeks might be a pain for the GM and will not allow much time for accomplishments. The GM might forget about you if the meetings are only once a month.

In these 10-minute meetings, you will go over what you have done in the *past* two weeks and what you will do in the *next* two weeks. These check-in meetings are an essential part of your plan because they allow your GM to see you making successful and continuous progress. They will make your GM feel invested in your accomplishments, and ultimately change his perception of you.

At this meeting, you've made commitments that will determine whether you can successfully change your GM's perceptions of you. Not only do you have to meet those commitments, but you must meet each one of them.

> **WARNING!** If for any reason you do not follow through on even one of your promised tasks, there won't be a second chance.

Tip It is crucial that you come across as realizing that there is a gap between your GM's expectations and your performance. To bridge this gap, you must have a sincere desire and commitment to change. The GM must believe that you are able to change your behavior and attitude.

Practice

Rehearse the meeting. You must appear firm and calm, with a clear recognition that there is a problem. You also must have a concrete plan–– one that will help to overcome your GM's negative perception of your performance.

Let's revisit the earlier situation. If you had first planned and rehearsed the meeting with the GM, using role play, you might have fared very differently. Role play is an excellent tool because it allows you to edit, project, and edit again. It is like the difference between writing and speaking. When you write, you can look at what you have typed, think about it for a while, and make careful revisions before the reader sees it. But when you speak, you are immediately committed to what you've said, so the words must be right the first time.

Find someone you trust who can play the role of GM. Choose someone who can be tough. Brief the person on your GM's temperament and tendencies so that the role play will be as realistic as possible. For the role play to be effective, your practice GM needs to listen not only to *what* you are saying but also to *how* you are saying it. Make sure they don't go easy on you in the role play because that will not help you.

Many managers put off this meeting because they are afraid of the consequences.

I have always found that it is the fear of the unknown that causes stress. The best way to NOT be nervous is to find out, not delay. Sometimes, the results aren't as bad as you thought they were. But, even if they are, at least you know what you must do.

Bottom line – find out sooner, rather than later.

Don't be afraid to come across as firm, but not aggressive, but you definitely don't want to come across as apologetic. No one wants to see a weak manager, especially in a serious meeting that is meant to get the GM's confidence, not lessen it. The GM wants to hear from a *determined* manager-- one who cares about the job and has a plan to succeed.

"Bob, I need to talk to you about something. It's really important to me and I need to resolve it." You need to be taken seriously. Look at GM in a direct way. I said, "OK, we're going back to the beginning, you're coming into the office, I'm busy looking over my papers, and I say, "Morning Michael, what's on your mind?"

"I have something I need to talk over with you," he said in a confident voice. "I've been thinking a lot about the way that I believe you see me. I have a plan that I would like to go over with you that will change that."

You want to sound firm, confident, and poised. You want the GM to sit up and want to listen. Remember, the GM has negative perceptions blocking what you have to say. You need to come across as having put a lot of thought and commitment into what you are saying. This is an important meeting and you've got to come across knowing this.

One of the questions that your GM will probably ask is if you like working here. It is an important question; one you should ask yourself. If you have doubts about whether you really want this job, it will be obvious to your GM. It is easy to go through the motions, work on autopilot, doing just enough to do the job, but with no real passion or plan. When that occurs, skip the meeting, it's time for a change.

Remember Practice. Practice. Practice.

GET THE MEETING

Two questions to answer to get the meeting:

- When is the best time to ask your GM for a meeting?

- What is the best approach?

The best time to approach the GM is when he or she will be alone for a few minutes. Do not follow the GM and ask, "do you have a minute?" This sounds like a casual request which is exactly the opposite of how you want to come across. Choose a time that you know the GM will be alone for at least a few minutes.

The best approach has you coming across as serious and that this meeting is important. You might say that you'd like a private meeting when it is convenient. You've got some important things you'd like to discuss that might take a while. You know the GM is busy, but this is important to you. You'd like to have a period of time that you could talk just the two of you uninterrupted.

You know the flow of a restaurant and you know when the best times are. For a meeting like this, it can be difficult to hold the meeting in the restaurant. The only exception is if another manager can be present, so that the GM and you can have uninterrupted time and the other manager is strong enough to make it happen.

Another option is to email the GM. If your GM uses email and more importantly reads their email, this is a good option. Email offers you the opportunity to phrase the meeting request so that it conveys your sincere desire to have a private meeting and that it is important to you. Make sure you ask for a period of time that will be uninterrupted.

It is important to convey that this is an important meeting to you. Don't treat it casually. This is a time to be diplomatic, yet forceful: "I have something that I need to talk to you about. I'd like to schedule a meeting with you when we can talk. This is really important to me."

WARNING! Even though your GM will probably schedule the meeting sometime in the future, be prepared that he might say "Let's go," and the meeting will start immediately. Because this is a real possibility, especially if your GM tends to make quick decisions, you must be mentally prepared to go right into the meeting.

To recap:

• Describe the situation - let the GM know that you understand he is not pleased with your performance.

• State why it is important to change his view of you.

• Specify what you want to happen.

• Discuss why this will be good for the company and you

• Propose regular dates to check in.

THE PURPOSE

You intend to change the GM's negative perception of you with superior and consistent performance.

Remember You are trying to get your GM to "buy-In" and to be personally invested in your turnaround. If you follow through with your plan, your relationship with the GM will change and you will be back on track. But, if for *any* reason you don't follow through, dust off your resume because you're toast. It won't matter what reason, even a legitimate reason, caused you to not follow through. There will be no second chances. Don't even ask. Update your resume.

WHAT WOULD YOU DO?

You arrive at your new restaurant excited, ready, and eager to do a great job.

But, after a while, you find that the General Manager ignores you and gives you the worst schedules. When you make a suggestion, the GM kind of listens, but nothing ever happens. At weekly manager meetings, you're basically ignored, never given any projects to do, never asked any questions.

You thought you were good at your job, but you also know

your GM no longer thinks so. You could tell that your standing with the GM had deteriorated over the past few months and he had even blasted you a couple of times in meetings. For days after meetings, you would try to avoid the GM as much as possible. The other assistant managers seemed to have good relationships with the GM, while you received no feedback, no praise, not even criticism.

You are surprised and disappointed because you never thought that this could happen to you. You love your job and your employees, so you shake it off and get to work, still determined to do a great job.

But, after a few more months, you find that nothing has changed. You think you are doing a good job, but you are now getting depressed and sometimes angry. You thought this situation would get better, but after several months, you're not sure if you can take it anymore. You find yourself not caring and you know you're not doing a good job because it doesn't seem to matter if you do a good job or bad job.

You've thought about quitting and looking for another job. You still like and believe in the company and would like to stay, but you're not sure what to do. You know that you must do something. You cannot continue like this, you dread the thought of a face-to-face meeting, but you force yourself to do it.

WHAT I DID

Once I made the decision to have the meeting, I began to doubt myself. Was I as good as I thought I was I just imagining being ignored?

Before I went to the GM, I had to figure out where I was. So, I evaluated myself as objectively and as brutally as possible. I had to make sure I was doing as good a job as I thought I was.

I went through my P&L responsibilities and made notes on which areas I was doing well, and which ones were just ok.

I made a list of my accomplishments during the past period that were over and above just running shifts. I also made a list of specific instances where I felt ignored.

I talked to the other assistants for advice.

After all that, I made a formal appointment with my GM. I had to know what was going on. If it went well, I would stay. If it went badly, I would know that I needed to look for another job.

By this time, I wasn't stressed, I was angry. I knew I was prepared for the meeting and I was ready to know where my future was heading.

REFLECTION

In hindsight, the only thing I would do differently would be to have the meeting much earlier. Because I delayed confronting the issue, my stress grew each day by worrying more and more, making me depressed and almost physically ill. I could have avoided all that by having a meeting as soon as I felt ignored.

The meeting went surprisingly well. The GM was a little surprised at how upset I appeared but seemed impressed by the level of preparation I had made.

We covered my P&L responsibilities, going over each line. He was surprisingly patient and engaged.

I was able to point out several accomplishments that he was unaware of or had forgotten about. Next, I brought up my perception of how the GM treated me. I brought up several specific instances where I felt ignored. Surprisingly, he was candid and actually offered an apology (of sorts). He claimed that he had no idea that I was being ignored. He said that he had noticed that I had been passive and quieter recently. Now he understood why. He promised to be more aware of his actions and reassured me that I was doing a good job and was on track for promotion. I felt this was the first time that the GM treated me as an equal. The meeting answered my question of whether to stay or leave. I just should have done this sooner.

PART 4

Tomorrow is Almost Here

CHAPTER 10

CAREER PLAN

You can do this

Many managers trust too much. They trust that if they come to work every day they will eventually be promoted. That is simply not true. Just coming to work will cause you to be passed over for promotions by other assistant managers who are aware of what they must do.

There is no one more interested in your career than you. If you don't make it a priority, no one else is going to. Career planning is really thinking about the end result first and then figuring out how to get there.

When I was a manager trainee and assistant manager, I was one of the ones who trusted too much. I relied on my GM and the company to figure out my development. I didn't see the "big picture", I just concentrated on each step that was put before me. I was naïve to do that and I'm sure it took me months longer to get promoted to GM.

Your career plan is to help you to achieve a personally satisfying and successful career.

On your first day, you start to establish your reputation, which is why the patterns and habits that you develop early are so important and powerful to your career.

THE START OF YOUR CAREER

The first phase of your career (manager trainee and assistant manager) is technical (learning how to do the tasks of employees who report to you and the tasks of managers (budgets, problem solving, managing shifts, ordering, making deposits, plus hundreds of others). Your career starts at manager trainee, advances to assistant manager, then on to GM.

This book concentrates on your journey to GM because I think that the promotion to GM is the most difficult promotion. Assistant managers, for a very large part, must rely on the GM for their advancement. GM's have the advantage that their performance is judged by their direct boss based on the performance of the restaurant without relying on a middleman (the GM in the assistant manager's case) for advancement.

MANAGE YOUR OWN GROWTH

If you don't have a plan, you're allowing yourself to go wherever, rather than where *you* want to go. I've noticed over the years that there are some assistant managers who "wait to be developed," while other assistant managers seem to control their careers, know where they want to go, and how to get there. GM's love this second kind of manager and do everything they can to support them.

Your career plan lays out the steps necessary to get promoted to the next level. You're not trying to rush, but you are trying to be efficient and avoid detours.

Who goes up fastest? The managers who get noticed are the ones who push themselves or are pushed by their mentors.

—RUSS BENDEL, CEO HABIT BURGER

ON A ROAD TRIP

Think about your career as you would a road trip. First you have a destination. You don't just get in your car and drive hoping you arrive where you want to go when you don't even know where you want to go.

What is the approximate time that it will take to go from manager trainee to assistant and from assistant manager to GM? Restaurant companies are usually very up front about how long it might take to make GM. With mature companies that are not growing it might take several years to make GM, while others, high growth chains, might want you to be ready for promotion is as little as a year. You've got to have your expectation be on the same page as the company.

What experience do you need to advance to each level? Once you find this out, make sure you are on a straight line to get those experiences.

Communicate regularly to your GM about what you should be doing and learning that would help you. Find out how you are perceived. Does your GM think you are weak in a particular area, such as food or kitchen? Do they think you could be more organized? Too close to your employees?

Find out! Even if you are given regular performance evaluations, ask for a meeting to discuss what your boss' perception is of you so that you can work on them. Make SURE that you communicate that your goal is to be promoted and that is the standard that you want to be measured by, even if you are a brand-new manager in training. Keep the bar high.

Without knowing how your boss perceives you, it is impossible to get better.

Remember that it is not how you are doing in your **current** job that is key to your promotion. It is whether your boss thinks that you can handle the next level that is important. For example, just because a cook is efficient and fast does not mean he would be a good manager. For the cook to be promotable, he would need to demonstrate reliability, able to handle different situations, not temperamental, respected, and able to grasp costs, scheduling, and many other aspects of the kitchen. In other words, the cook would have to be seen as someone who could be a manager.

MANAGER TRAINEE

At first, the restaurant can be overwhelming because it seems so huge. It has so many more moving parts than you ever imagined. Dishwashers, bussers, prep, servers, hosts, cooks, bartenders, bar backs, recipes, controls, expenses, sales, net income, cost of sales, operating income, labor costs, budget variance, equipment, security, policies, procedures, health inspectors, deposits, overages, shortages, standards, cleanliness, morale, and of course, those pesky customers.

Training usually ranges from none to 6 months with 3 months being the average. This training period is usually set with little negotiation possible. As a manager trainee, your goal is to learn each position in the restaurant: Busser, host, bartender, server, cook, prep, dishwasher, cashier, etc.

This is **not** the time to show how much you know. In fact, relax a bit since this is the ONLY time in your restaurant career that it is ok to NOT know. Even if you think you know, ask anyway. No one expects you to know everything. In fact, you'll be a total jerk if you give the impression that you do.

Ask questions of each position trainer. "Why do you do it that way?" "How do you know when it is ready?" Be humble and be a sponge. Your trainers are good at their positions; remember, they do it every day, so you'll probably never be as good, or at least you'll never be as fast. That's ok, you don't need to be. Make a point to get to know each employee a little at a time when you work with them by asking questions. Chances are that each employee can do their job better than you can, so respect that.

I suggest you cool your competitive urges. Your job is to learn how to do each position well, not win a competition that isn't there. Since speed comes with practice, don't think you suck just because you are so much slower than they are. Make sure you compliment them when you see them do well. It is far more important for you to know how to do each job well, not fast. You need to know each technique so that you can step in, evaluate, or train.

You don't have to have all the answers.

WHEN YOU START AS NEW ASSISTANT MANAGER

Most importantly do a good job as manager. You'll get more respect quickly by simply doing your job and doing it well. When you first get there, I suggest that you don't change anything for a while. Resist the temptation to "hit the ground running" until you've got a thorough overview. The reason is that you probably don't know as much as you think you do.

Your first priority is to master each area of the restaurant. You will spend a period of time in charge of one area then be moved to be in charge of another area (Servers, bussers and hosts/esses, Bar, kitchen) until you understand and master scheduling, costs, training, and motivations of required of each department. Believe it or not, each are very different.

Before you go to the GM to make your case that you are ready to move to another area, make sure your area is staffed, trained, with good morale, and that your labor costs are within budget. Once you think you have mastered an area, go to the GM to discuss if the GM agrees that you are ready to move to another area. Don't try to rush each area, but don't just sit back and wait and wait for the GM to make it happen either. Sometimes you've got to push (I mean remind) the GM.

Your choice: the player who sits on the bench waiting to be called in to the game or the player who goes to the coach and says, "Put me in!"

Pay attention to the GM and the other assistant managers when they make decisions or handle different situations. Would you have done it the same way? Even if you wouldn't, file it away.

To establish yourself as promotable, it takes more than showing up, doing your job, and doing it again. You are establishing your reputation as promotable.

> **It takes the 3 I's to get ahead:**
> *Integrity, Intelligence, and Intensity—each with herculean effort*
> -JERRY HENNESSY, CO-FOUNDER OF STACKED AND BJ'S RESTAURANTS

ADVANCED ASSISTANT MANAGER

Once you've grasped each of the areas, concentrate on the big picture. This includes understanding the many aspects of a great guest experience and the many systems that are in a restaurant. You are trying to take on larger roles at each stage of your development and differentiating yourself from the other assistant managers by establishing yourself as a manager who has a pattern of success.

It is critical that you understand the P&L backwards and forwards, how to control the P&L in each area and understand the priorities of running the entire restaurant.

**HERE'S HOW YOU CAN HELP YOURSELF AT THIS
STAGE OF YOUR CAREER:**

1. Diversity and adversity beat repetition

> *Have you had 3 years of experience or
> have you had 1 year of experience 3 times?*

Don't be afraid to go after difficult jobs. T best learning happens with the more difficult the job, the more outside your comfort zone you get, the worse the personnel problem, the most severe profit pressure, and the most difficult employees.

Even though these all sound like they suck (and they do!), you'll learn the most. You can't stay in your comfort zone to get better. You're trying to get yourself ready for taking on larger and larger roles and responsibilities.

2. Own it. Hold yourself and your employees accountable.

Keep your standards high and consistent. Whether you think you are or not, you are a role model. Everything you say and do are important. If you want your employees to help each other, you're the one who must do it consistently and enforce it.

Your employees absolutely and positively know which managers they can get over. Don't be one of them. You may think that being easy and slack gets you liked. It won't and you lose all respect. The employees who like this kind of manager are not the kind you want.

*3. Be a student of learning how to influence your employee's
behavior and team behavior.*

This starts with a genuine caring for your employees. What do they require to be successful? Why are they working at your restaurant? Find out and make sure that you have done everything possible so that they are successful. The number one reason why employees quit is because management does not care.

4. Seek out developmental assignments for skills growth

Volunteer to take charge of a new corporate initiative or learn one of the restaurant systems in-depth, like programming, or any that you are uncomfortable with. Once you dig in, you'll most likely be amazed at how much you like it. Few people like what they can't do well. The first time you picked up a guitar, you weren't good at it. It wasn't easy. But, if you kept practicing, you got better and better.

5. Make sure you learn from your experiences.

Ask yourself, "What would I do differently?" If something happens that is negative, ask yourself, "How could I prevent it from happening again? What were the signs that I could have seen but ignored?

6. Observe how other managers react to different situations.

This can be a tremendous learning opportunity when you allow yourself to stop, step back, and reflect thoughtfully on an event. This allows you to absorb and learn. If you don't understand the why, ask the manager what led to their decision.

7. When you start each position, make sure you understand your job, your responsibilities, and your authority.

WHAT IF I'M OFFERED A TRANSFER?

When I started out in management, I was transferred 5 times within 5 years. At the time, it was exciting. I was led to believe that the path to promotion definitely led through transfer.

The question, upon reflection, was how many of the moves actually improved my career? Today, I would say that probably only one of the 5 actually did. The rest were best for the company, but not particularly for me. Did they lie? Were they intentionally misleading me? No, I don't think so. I think they sincerely believed they would remember my willingness to sacrifice personally for the good of the company.

Transfers are tough. You and your family are the ones who must deal with the hassles of selling and buying a house, renting another apartment, wife changing jobs, kids changing schools, and leaving friends and relatives behind, etc.

The message is that you should never blindly accept transfers because, unfortunately, some "opportunities" actually turn out to be lateral moves that benefit your employer, not you.

The problem of course, is that these "opportunities" sound so good, especially when your supervisor has made a big deal about meeting you. They set up a special meeting and seem so excited about your "opportunity"; looks you right in the eye and says sincerely "this will be great for your career and we appreciate your doing this".

You will receive several of these new and exciting sounding opportunities during your career. But you must examine them with objective detachment and the viewpoint of the opportunity's significance to your goal as well as the impact it has on your family.

Ask your boss a few questions:

Why will it be great for my career?
Is it because
- it is an opening? New experience, more opportunity.

- it is a new concept? New experience, more opportunity.

- it is a major leap in sales? Bigger bonus.

- It is a promotion? More responsibility, bigger salary and bonus.

WHY will it be great?

Have them tell you why it is NOT just a lateral move. It should be more than just more money too because with most transfers, if you must physically move from where you live, you will lose money.

After you have all the information about the 'whys' of the move, tell your boss you appreciate them choosing you and you'd like a day or two to think about it.

Then go to your significant other and see what he or she thinks about this. I made a mistake when I accepted a transfer when my baby girl was just 3 weeks old. It placed a terrible strain on my wife and I still regret the move to this day. I should have just said no, the timing was not right.

Remember that ALL good companies will respect your decision to turn down a transfer, unless it is part of their culture that you should have known when you first joined. It is always a good idea to communicate your position to move with your supervisor at the sooner, not later.

Each time you move, there are costs above and beyond dollars.

- My wife had to quit her job, which meant that she had to start over at another job. She had to apply, get hired, and fit in once again, all highly emotional drains. Plus, it meant an interruption in her pay, which is always bad. Also, by constantly having new jobs, she was never able to have any job become a satisfying career.

- We bought 3 houses within that period of time. Two houses owned for less than two years and one for only a year which meant we made a total of zero appreciation. Other managers, who were not being "promoted", had houses that appreciated.

Later, when I was vice president of operations of a chain myself, some transfers weren't for my managers' career development, but filling slots, so I gave them raises to compensate. Few really pressed me to explain how the moves were good for them, but you should.

Any wisdom from this? Maybe. Here are some points to consider:

• Before you accept any transfer, the first question to ask is how this move will help your professional development. If the move really is in your best interests, your supervisor will have no problem explaining the logic of the transfer. If it turns out to be a lateral move with nothing to gain, turn it down unless you just want to have a change of scenery or the company makes it worth your while.

• Consider all the expenses involved. Is the company picking up the cost of deposits, moving expenses, house hunting trip, mileage, and other miscellaneous expenses? Remember to consider the hassle and time needed to buy and sell a house, give notice, clean out your apartment, look at other apartments, your significant other's career plans, friends left behind, plus any emotional attachment to your present location.

• Will there be a significant pay increase if you accept the transfer?

• ALWAYS, check with your significant other to see if the move fits the family's overall game plan.

The bottom line is for you to take charge of your career. After all, if you don't, who will?

WHAT WOULD YOU DO?

You are a new assistant manager in charge of the servers at a full-service restaurant. You were volunteered to be in charge of the new service program that corporate is rolling out.

One of your long-term servers is resisting the new system and is becoming quite negative and vocal about it. She is complaining so much about the new server program that is causing other servers to be reluctant to want to be a part of it.

She says that she has been very successful waiting tables for the past 2 years and that her tips are above average and has many call customers. She doesn't need or want the new system.

What would you do?

WHAT I DID

I was tempted to take the easy way to just tell her to do it or else. But the reality is that I didn't want to lose a good, long term employee. So, I tried a different tactic.

I went to her to ask for her help. If I could persuade her to buy in and help, she could influence the other servers to accelerate the training program, rather than hurt it.

First, I told her that I was aware that she didn't think too much of the new service program. I explained that corporate had tested this program at other units and that it had caused service to improve and that tips had gone up as well, even with very good servers, like herself.

I told her that she was one of our best servers and if she would give the training program a chance, I'd like to make her a trainer. I'd pay her more for being a trainer and that her experience and influence would go a long way in helping other servers increase their tips.

In this case, she did give it a chance, became a trainer, and in this case at least, she became a believer in the program.

REFLECTION

This time it worked. But, if she had turned me down, I would have been forced to tell her that I expect her to follow the new service program and to keep her comments to herself. If she did not, there would be consequences.

> **WARNING:** NEVER tell employees that you don't like or don't agree with any new system, but you have to go along with it. When you do this, your employees will resist even more accepting new procedures and you will have compromised all management. If (when) your GM hears what you said, you'll be toast.

CHAPTER 11

WHAT'S HOLDING YOU BACK?

When to leave and when to stay

Sometimes it may seem like you're just not getting anywhere. You're pulling shifts, working hard, but you sense that your career has stopped moving forward. Others have gotten promoted, but you're still just pulling shifts. What's going on?

THE DREADED LOOP

The new manager starts with a new company. Excited. Gung ho. Goes through management training program and becomes an assistant manager. Works hard. Then one day realizes that there is no hope for getting promoted. Looks for a better opportunity with another company. Resigns from company, starts at new company. Goes through management training program and becomes an assistant manager. Works hard. Then one day realizes that there is no hope for promotion.

Repeat.

Whoa! Something is wrong.

If you just can't seem to get promoted to GM, if you're stuck at assistant manager, if you keep changing jobs, it's time to take a hard look at yourself, your career, and your future. You've got to get out of this loop.

Maybe it's the wrong type of company for you, or maybe it's the GM, or maybe, just maybe, the restaurant industry is trying to tell you something. Regardless of the reason, you can't keep doing this.

SO, LET'S EXPLORE WHAT MAY BE GOING ON.

I've found that there are four levels of frustration:

- GM

- Company

- Restaurant environment, but maybe some other foodservice would work if one exists (You hate to throw away so much experience)

- The entire restaurant and foodservice industry

GM

I think anyone who has been in the business world longer than one job has experienced the wrong boss. By wrong GM, I mean one who has a different management style, or one you can't communicate with, or just cannot get along with, or just incompetent.

My particular problem with my GM was with management styles. I remember one GM I had. She managed with a classic crisis management style. She would whirl around the restaurant like a leaf in a dust storm telling people to do this, go there, and clean that. She had a very difficult time with anyone who did not have this Type A personality. How could anyone possibly be doing a good job without running around?

My style of management was the opposite. Calmer, planned, and hardly ever Type A. Believe it or not, we had a difficult time together. Actually, that's not true. *I* had the difficult time. After all, as she reminded me often, **she** was the GM.

This difference in management style would have been fine if she could have seen that they both can work. It is the effectiveness of management that should be judged, not how you get there. The experience went a long way toward my trying to look beyond surface differences to focus on results.

If you find yourself experiencing this same kind of clash, the best thing to do is first talk to your GM. But don't do it in an informal way. Don't do it casually-right-in-the-middle-of-the-busy-part-of-the-shift. Request a meeting that will be private with no interruptions. You want your GM to know that you are serious, that there is something bothering you, and you need to resolve it.

Describe the situation to your GM, just as you see it, but do it with a twist. First, describe the situation, but do it with the assumption that your GM *wants* you to perform well. Do not criticize the way the GM runs the shift in any way. Start off with something like, "I know you want me to be the best manager I can be because you want your restaurant to be the best."

"I also want this to be the best restaurant and I want to be the best manager, but I'm concerned about our relationship and I'd like to talk to you about it."

Be honest about what is troubling you and agree on management development talks to discuss the pros and cons of doing things. You'll learn things here and, hopefully, if your GM has even a partial open mind, he or she will too.

If things go badly and communication is nonexistent between the two of you, go to your GM and say that you would like to transfer. You'll have to make the decision based on your relationship with your district manager (your GM's boss) whether you try to transfer out of your supervisor's area also.

WARNING: Do NOT go to your GM's boss without letting the GM know first. Often, jumping the chain of command can be career suicide. Communicating honestly is the key in the long term, but it is tough in the short term.

When your boss is incompetent, difficult, or just not that good.

Whether it's due to poor people skills, inexperience, or a lack of managerial aptitude, an incompetent manager can hurt your career. While this will require you to grit your teeth and sometimes go into the walk-in to scream, these strategies will help turn the GM from your worst enemy into a supporter.

• **Take a deep breath:** you've gotten a bad deal. Having an incompetent boss can be frustrating when we think that we could do the job better. But what you've got is your reality, so make the best of it. The good news is that you can. Put yourself in your boss's shoes. How would you feel if you were elevated into a position that you weren't qualified for? How would you want your team to treat you?

• **Where's the incompetence?** It is worth spending some time figuring out where the incompetence is. Does the GM play favorites so much so that it hurts the efficiency and morale of the restaurant? Is it from lack of experience? While there are hundreds of reasons why someone is incompetent, make sure that your opinion of the GM is not due to just having a different management approach or different style than you.

• **Compensate and cover:** Once you've pinpointed the major deficiencies, make and enact strategies to compensate. Yes, this requires extra effort. No, this isn't fair. But letting an incompetent boss derail your career isn't fair either. Look for opportunities to shine by doing great work and becoming your boss's biggest asset. Find opportunities to compensate for your boss's weakness. Offer to cover for her when she is out. Proactively provide information that will help him. Offer to take on more responsibility and projects. Use your interactions to help teach them what they need to know.

• **Take the long view:** Try not to worry if your boss gets the credit for your successful projects. Success gets noticed, and in organizations that usually means the team and/or department gets noticed too. Make your boss and your team look good and you will look good as well. Plus, people aren't stupid—everyone probably already knows that you are the success engine behind your incompetent boss.

• **Learn what you can:** If your boss is technically competent, take the time to learn about her technical expertise. Use this opportunity to hone your technical skills.

FEELING OVERWHELMED

• If you feel intense pressure whenever you start thinking about work, it is time to stop and ask yourself why. In almost every case it is the fear of the unknown. So, ask yourself what is it that you are worried about? What is it that you don't know?

• Concerned about your job performance?

• Worried about being terminated?

• Worried about not being promoted?

• Concerned with the performance of your area of responsibility?

• Health issue?

• Personal issue?

• Family issue?

• Whatever the problem, the best advice is to address the question and find an answer to it. In most cases, once you confront an issue and find out how bad it really is, will relieve your anxiety because you'll know, not just worry about the unknown. You'll feel energized when you find out. Just dwelling on something only makes it worse.

• If it is a performance issue, think about it. Make an appointment with your general manager. But before the meeting, do your homework. What do YOU think you are doing well and not so well? When you talk with the GM, let him/her know you are aware of the problems and that you have a plan to correct them. Address the problem areas with specific plans for each area to do a better job. No boss (no effective boss) can criticize you for knowing and correcting problems. Your boss has a legitimate gripe with you when you do not know your problem areas or/and you have no plan to correct them.

• If it is a personal/health/family matter talk it out. Think about the worst-case scenario. After that is on the table, you'll know where you stand. Just recognizing that fact usually makes you realize that even in the worst case, you will survive and many times you will be wiser and in a better position.

• The bottom line is that feeling overwhelmed is usually caused by something that is unknown. This is usually brought on by not wanting to deal with some problem. But the longer you put it off, the worse it gets. It is natural to not want to deal with something unpleasant, but this is the cause of feeling overwhelmed. Once you sit down and deal with it, you will feel better because you have turned the unknown into the known.

FEELING UNDER WHELMED

• Are you bored? Do you feel you are on autopilot while at work? Are you just going through the motions?

- I've been there and it isn't fun. If you are feeling bored, the problem is that you ARE bored. One result of boredom and being on autopilot is that you are not doing your best work. Not even close. Another is that you are not looking long term at all. Your definition of long term is, at best, tomorrow. Your standards go way down, and you overlook actions of employees that you would once have written up in a heartbeat.

- But no one will notice right? I mean you're good. You can do your job blindfolded.

- No, you can't. You're going to get noticed. If you have a great GM, he or she will counsel you and try to help figure out what is going on with you. If you have an average GM, you will get fired. And you know what? You deserve it.

- Your GM, your company and certainly you do not deserve to give anything less than 100 percent while at work. It is not personally satisfying for you and it is not productive for your company. It is time to take a long hard look at what is wrong.

- You need a challenge that you're not experiencing in your present job. You need to do something. Talk it out with a close friend, your wife, husband, significant other, or maybe even your GM. Drastic changes may not be called for, such as leaving the company or industry, but some change is.

- Perhaps you need to change responsibilities in your restaurant. Go from being over the servers to the kitchen, for example. It might be a great time to ask for a transfer to a new city that you are interested in. Or it would be a great time in your career to be one of the managers at a new opening if one is scheduled in the near future.

- But I would guess that the root problem is something else entirely. I would bet that you are feeling ignored. Actions that you have taken in the past, the ones in which you worked hard and

were justifiably proud of your accomplishments, were not noticed. When this inattention is repeated, it is human nature to
feel fed up and not try anymore. Why bother to work hard? No
one notices anyway.

• Before you toss in the towel and relax your standards to the
point that you hurt your reputation, try this first. Think about
the real reasons behind feeling underwhelmed and bored. It just
might be a lack of feedback.

• Talk it out with someone. Then go to your GM. Explain
that you need more feedback, and you would like to set goals for
tasks and achievements with dates for reviews. This way you have
forced feedback (in a professional way). Once you have done this
for a period of time, you should be ready to present your case to
be promoted or to a new situation. Try it. You'll like it.

I HATE MY COMPANY

For whatever reason, you chose the wrong company. To solve
this, you've got to know what is most important to you.

What do you require most from a job? Is it prestige, money, advancement, location, job security, or benefits? Your priority
will vary over time and circumstances, of course, but matching
your priority with a company may the most important aspect to
your job satisfaction. For example, if advancement is your priority, you'll want a company that is growing. But maybe you just
couldn't resist a job offer from a company that had so much prestige that you just couldn't say no. Trust me on this, you'll soon
quit because this job did not and could not satisfy your primary
requirement of promotion. Before you just get another job with
another company, take the time to look inward to make sure you
know what is most important. Then find a match.

Sometimes it is simply the wrong place

I once thought that I could live anywhere. I suppose I got that attitude because I grew up in a military family. My dad was transferred about every 3 years and so the family would say adios to friends and look forward to a new adventure. It never bothered me to move and I think it helped me to adapt to different situations easier.

My first restaurant management job was with Steak and Ale way back when the earth was cooling. I was transferred 5 times within 5 years. Too many times, for sure, but as far as the places we were transferred to, there was never any problems. All good. We loved each place. All the transfers just confirmed our belief that any place could be great. All it required was a good attitude.

However, I found that was not entirely true. I left Steak and Ale to go to what I thought at the time to be a better opportunity for myself, my wife, and family. This new opportunity was in a completely different part of the country. But no problem, I took the job thinking that we could live anywhere. I thought it would be just another adventure for my family to experience together and enjoy. We were positive we'd learn to love it as much as anywhere.

I'm not sure if it was the job or the place, but everything was wrong. The people were negative. The weather was bad, and my job was terrible. To this day, I'm not sure what influenced the other more. Did my not liking the city spill over into my job or did my negative attitude of my job create a bad attitude about the city? Just about one year to the day, I quit the job, accepted another job and moved to another city.

The bottom line is that I no longer believe that anyplace will always be a good place. I have lived in six different states, both coasts of the US, and considerable time living overseas. I have loved 90% of the places where I have lived, but there are some places that just did not feel right. It is important to recognize that there must be a good fit with where you live. I now believe that feeling good about where you live is necessary to have a good attitude about life in general and your job specifically.

When you are considering accepting a transfer or a new job in a new city, consider the following:

• Any move must be a joint, mutually agreed upon decision with your wife/husband/partner. The move must be a win-win with your significant other. If things go bad, you will need your partner's support. Even if the transfer is for a significant promotion or increase in pay, slow down and talk it out. The last thing either of you need is for the other to say that they didn't want to go in the first place. Don't bully your significant other or be bullied into a move that is not right. There will be other jobs and other opportunities, I promise.

• Listen to your gut feel. If things don't feel right, they probably aren't right. Your gut feel is made up of your experiences so listen to it.

• If you don't know anything about the new place, give it a chance by seeing the whole area as much as possible. Travel to the scenic spots, read the local newspaper, spend some time at parks, hang out at the local coffee place and just observe. How does it feel? Do you like the energy? Do you feel you could be a part of this?

• Match the location with your interests. Is Florida the best place for you if you love to ski and hate to fly? If you love culture, restaurants, ethnic diversity, theater and shopping that a big city has to offer, you're probably not ready for a small town, no matter how great the job is. And vice versa. No matter how great the job in a big urban city, you will soon hate it if you are not prepared to use public transit or commute. And sometimes a long commute.

I am very much for moving to different areas of the country and the world, but I know now that there are some places I would rather visit than live. It is better to know before you commit rather than after.

WHEN IT'S SO AWFUL, SO BAD, SO TERRIBLE THAT YOU THINK YOU'VE GOT TO LEAVE THE RESTAURANT INDUSTRY

Could it be that you have had it with the restaurant industry itself with the crazy hours, working weekends and holidays, but you like the employees and the food areas? Plus, and this is a big, giant plus, you really don't want to go to another industry because you've learned so much about employees and foodservice.

Before you leave the foodservice industry, you owe it to yourself to look at options that you may not have thought about within the foodservice industry.

There are many opportunities in foodservice that you may not know about and one of them may be perfect for you. You may not realize it, but you have acquired a tremendous amount of technical knowledge, expertise, and experience that will be completely transferable in another part of foodservice. Each area has a completely different environment, career path, hours, days, responsibilities, and opportunities, but they all share food and people as their core. You owe it to yourself to check it out.

Two of the largest are Sodexo and Aramark, but there are others, as well as independents. Here's a short profile on each. A couple of excellent resources to explore are www.food-management.com and www.cmaa.org (Club Managers Association of America).

Some examples:

• University – If you enjoy an academic setting, then consider university foodservice. You'll be responsible for student dorms and a student center with many quick service restaurants. But that's not all. If the university has sports, there will be stadiums to service, plus many have a faculty club with a full-service restaurant. During the summer, it slows way down. Universities are closed during extended holidays like Christmas, closed during spring break, and closed on most national holidays.

• K-12 – This possibly has the shortest number of working days in the year since schools are closed during the summer and closed on most holidays and weekends. You'll work in a school district with many schools. Lots of paperwork because of requirements to meet dietary and federal guidelines and regulations.

• Hospital/health care – in charge of patients, visitors, and health care staff food service. Sometimes, there is a foodservice professional who is in charge and sometimes it is a Registered Dietitian.

• Corporate – This is defined as any company that does not have food service as its primary business, such as Google, IBM, or Ford Motors. Often, there is no foodservice during weekends and evenings. The environment is usually the same as the corporate culture, meaning some are formal and some are casual.

• Private clubs (Country club, yacht club, tennis club, city club) - Private clubs can be much more personal than restaurants, since you'll get to know the members and their families through daily interactions at the full and limited-service restaurants, and the many events (weddings, graduations, birthdays, tournaments, etc).

• Sports / entertainment- if you like complete chaos, followed by complete quiet, this might be for you. Think about a baseball game, for example. You have probably 30 different areas that serve hotdogs and beer, which all get slammed at the same time, then nothing, then slammed, then nothing. Plus, there are upscale restaurants and bars. The tough parts are that since games are not every day, most of your employees will be part timers with few full-time. So, the challenge is how to hire, train and retain many part timers. When there are no games, often these venues will also cater to concerts or other events.

• Correctional – a bit lacking in the prestige factor, but still one that you could explore.

• Military Officers club, NCO club, and Enlisted club: You will be a federal employee with all federal benefits such as 30 days off, ability to transfer anywhere in the world that has a US military base, and great retirement benefits. Most food service managers never think of this choice, but in many of my classes that compared all the options, this often came in first.

> *Nope, I just can't deal with it anymore.*
> *I've tried, but this just isn't for me.*

On my first job after college, before I found the restaurant industry, I had a job in manufacturing that was the wrong fit for me. At first, I liked the job because it was new, I could get a nicer apartment, and nicer car.

I felt vaguely unhappy all the time. Then one day I looked at my boss and realized that I didn't want his job. I realized that I cared absolutely zero about being promoted and knew this wasn't the place for me. From that point on, I felt better because I now had a mission, and that mission was to find a job and a career that I really wanted.

You may be experiencing the same things that I felt on that first job when I had to pull the plug.

• Are you just going through the motions, working on auto-pilot?

• Can you see yourself as your boss?

• Do you feel tired while at work?

• Are you always looking forward to your days off, dreading going back to work?

• Do you find yourself complaining to your friends about work?

• Do you have to catch yourself because your bad attitude might show?

Personally, I found the restaurant industry perfect. It had plenty of energy, variety, and opportunity; everything my first job didn't have. However, the restaurant industry might not be right for you.

If the above sounds like you, then you may be in the wrong industry. You'll be doing yourself, your GM, your friends, and family a favor if you accept that fact and start doing something about it. When you're in the right job, one that fits your own needs and future, you will be energized and a much happier person.

I'LL END WITH MY OWN
SHIFT FROM HELL

Have you ever had one of those days when you had a really rough shift and all you wanted to do was go home, grab a beer, turn on the TV, watch anything, and just unwind?

Yeah, me too

The story begins on a Friday nightbusy as hell, lines out the door, but it was going ok. No serious problems, except that we were a little shorthanded, so I had to buzz around quite a bit. I was really looking forward for the night to end. It was about a half hour before closing when I got a frantic tugging at my arm that the toilets had overflowed.

No problem. No big deal. I grabbed a busser, sent him in to clean it up, and forgot about it.

Then I got a report from the kitchen that the kitchen drains were all backing up and it was really getting wet in there. I go into the kitchen and sure enough, the floor was wet with water coming in through the drain lines. Lots of it. Fast. Did I say lots? Time for the plumber. I needed professional help now.

The water continued to rise. It didn't take long for the kitchen to be under 1 inch of water, then 2 inches. By now the water was starting to leak out into the dining room. Did I mention that this wasn't just water, but sewage water? Oh, yeah. And you can imagine that the water did not smell exactly great either.

I was in the kitchen with a mop when a hostess comes in to say that she was starting to get lots of complaints about the smell. Would I do something, please? The kitchen was totally flooded now with everyone just about ankle deep. The only one who was enjoying himself was the dishwasher, who loved that everyone was smelling and looking like he usually smelled and looked.

I turned around to talk to the hostess, when I slipped. Right into the muck. I fell totally flat. About a 9.3 in the new Olympic event of manager-slipping-in sewage-in-kitchen. I was sopping wet, not feeling real good. I was wet, frustrated, and smelly.

I couldn't leave to change since I was the only manager. I put on a cook's shirt from the office, which was too small because we had just given out all the larger ones. But, it was clean, which meant it was fine, even though it was really tight and looked ridiculous on me.

The plumber arrived late of course. By the time the plumber had finished, and I had mopped the kitchen by myself, (I had sent everyone home because it was so late), I was totally beat. It was around 3:30 AM in the morning. I finally got in my car to head home.

Little did I know that this night was just starting.

I was driving home when I spotted two guys next to a car who were trying to get someone to stop to help them.

I stopped.

What the hell; misery loves company. They said they had run out of gas and asked if I could give them a ride to a gas station? Sure, hop in. I drove to an all-night gas station. While I waited in the car, they went in to get some gas and coffee. As we drove back to their car with the gas, a police car gets in back of me, turns on its lights, and starts the siren right behind me.

I stopped.

He pulls out his gun and yells: "Get out and spread 'em!" It turns out that while my boys were in the gas station, they were also robbing the place. The gas station guy called the police and here we are!

It took a while before I convinced the policeman that I was not part of this entire deal, that I had just tried to help the hitch-hikers. The policeman said he had heard that one before, but the guys helped me and said the same thing. I then showed the policeman where I had picked them up by their (stolen) car.

I was finally allowed to go home. As I pulled up to my apartment, the paper was being delivered, the sun was coming up, and now a beer sounded better than a coffee.

Thanks for reading!

If this book has been of value to you,
I would greatly appreciate if you would leave a review.

Made in the USA
Las Vegas, NV
15 December 2022

62845808R00125